DUCHESS OF HAMILTON

AND THE

PRINCESS CORONATION CLASS

Another official works photograph taken in May 1938 apparently depicting Duchess of Hamilton. *It serves to emphasise the manner in which the 'speed stripes' complement the streamlined locomotive's impressive lines. However, this similarity between this and the photograph on page 33 (from another collection) appears to confirm earlier suspicions!*
                                        (1997-7397 DY 23915: NRM Collection)

Published by

Friends of the National Railway Museum Enterprises Ltd

First edition March 2009

AUTHOR: ROB ADAMSON

Few of Britain's longer railway routes were conceived as such; most resulted from combinations of smaller railways built at different times with money invested by private individuals, commercial organizations and financial institutions. Such combinations resulted from voluntary amalgamations, mergers and absorption of smaller companies by richer and more powerful neighbours. Whenever a planned railway required compulsory land purchase for its construction no progress was possible until Parliamentary approval had been received (in the form of an Act) and many proposed lines failed during the preliminary Committee stages. There was no overall national plan as the Government was committed to free enterprise and no public money was used directly to finance railway construction, although some railways were built to benefit from lucrative mail contracts. Many proposed mergers were rejected by Parliament as 'not being in the public interest' because unregulated route duplication was seen as the best form of competition.

The West Coast main line, referred to as such to differentiate from the rival East Coast route from London to Edinburgh through Peterborough, Doncaster, York and Newcastle, had its origins in the Liverpool & Manchester Railway opened in 1830. While the Stockton & Darlington Railway was the first public railway to be completed as a result of an Act of Parliament, it was never designed for exclusive use by steam locomotives as, in addition to rope haulage on the steepest inclines, much goods and most early passenger traffic were horse drawn. After trials held at Rainhill in October 1829, Liverpool & Manchester Railway directors were convinced that steam traction worked effectively and relatively efficiently and placed total reliance on steam locomotives for all traffic. The line was absorbed by the Grand Junction Railway in 1845.

A railway between London and Birmingham was considered at an earlier date but failed to receive Parliamentary approval. Following the Liverpool & Manchester's success a revised proposal was made in 1832 and the London & Birmingham Railway Act received Royal Assent in May 1833. With George and Robert Stephenson as engineers, work soon started on the 111-mile line from Camden Town to Birmingham (Curzon Street) which was opened throughout in September 1838. The railway went back to Parliament in 1835 for permission to build an extension from Camden to Euston Square, bringing its London terminus much closer to the city centre.

The Grand Junction Railway received Royal Assent on the same day in May 1833. This was an 83-mile extension from Birmingham to link with the Liverpool & Manchester Railway near to Newton-le-Willows (on early maps it appeared simply as Newton). It opened in July 1837 but its real importance began in 1838 when it became possible to travel by rail from London to Birmingham, Manchester or Liverpool. The Manchester & Birmingham Railway was authorized in 1837 but, starting from Manchester, it extended only as far as Crewe and in 1846 it merged with the London & Birmingham and Grand Junction Railways to form the London & North Western Railway (LNWR).

The Trent Valley Railway was authorized in 1845 as a more direct route between Stafford and Rugby (avoiding

No. 6220 Coronation *picks up water at speed at Dillicar troughs, near Tebay, while working the 'Coronation Scot'*   (Gresley Society).

No. 6220 Coronation *makes an impressive departure from Glasgow with the up 'Coronation Scot'* (Gresley Society)

Wolverhampton, Birmingham and Coventry) and the still incomplete railway was bought in 1846 (it opened throughout late 1847) by the London & Birmingham Railway on behalf of the new LNWR. This was a convoluted time in the history of the companies involved and the published histories are well worth reading; this recommendation applies equally well to the section from Crewe to Carlisle which, at one time, involved no less than six different railway companies. North from Carlisle the situation was less confused as there were only two competing routes; the Caledonian Railway opened its line between Glasgow and Carlisle via Annandale, Beattock and the Clyde Valley in 1849 and, for the first time, passengers were offered through journeys between London and Glasgow 'without change of carriage' although the 12½-hour trip in non-corridor coaches may have dissuaded more than a few potential customers. The Glasgow & South Western Railway, a bitter rival of the Caledonian throughout (and even beyond) its independent existence, opened its alternative route through Dumfries in 1850.

A significant factor that governed the way in which the West Coast main line operated was in the initial choice of civil engineer. Robert Stephenson engineered the London & Birmingham Railway and, other than a steep climb with a 1 in 66 gradient out of Euston to clear the bridge over the Regent's Canal at Camden (rope haulage powered by stationary condensing beam engines was employed for the first few years after opening) there were few northbound gradients more severe than 1 in 330 although the almost continuous climb from Camden to Tring (some 30 miles) made severe demands on both locomotives and firemen.

Joseph Locke (1805-1860) was apprenticed to George Stephenson (and remained a lifelong friend of

George's son Robert) but fell from favour with Stephenson senior when, at the Directors' request, he re-surveyed the tunnel workings of the Liverpool & Manchester Railway's extension from Crown Street to its projected new terminus at Lime Street and confirmed that opposing shafts would fail to meet unless realigned. After parting company from Stephenson, Locke practiced as an independent engineer and achieved considerable success through his ability to combine engineering and accounting skills, resulting in most of his railway construction contracts being completed within both time and budget. He worked with leading contractors of the time, notably Thomas Brassey (1805-1870) who, although employing as many as 75,000 men at the height of his career, was unusual as he ensured that all were treated fairly and with dignity. Much of Locke's success came from his reluctance to adopt expensive heavy engineering features and, paradoxically, while his independent career started because of his tunnelling expertise on both the Liverpool & Manchester and Canterbury & Whitstable Railways, he avoided tunnels on his own lines wherever possible. Locke established his Theory of Gradients which stated that while a level line is ideal, it should not be sought after if the interest on extra capital required for the necessary earthworks (achieved through tunnelling or embankment construction) exceeds expenditure on the extra fuel burnt when climbing gradients.

Joseph Locke engineered the main lines north from Lancaster which included the climb from Carnforth (some 6½ miles north of Lancaster) to Shap Summit, some 32 miles further north, with the final gradient increasing to 1 in 75. (Up to the last years of steam, banking engines were based at Tebay to assist trains, especially goods, in their final assault of the seven or so miles to the summit.)

5

No. 46223 Princess Alice *waits for its next turn of duty at Carlisle Station on 2 March 1967. While the class was designed to work the full distance between London (Euston) and Glasgow, it later became customary for locomotives on long-distance trains to be changed at either Crewe or Carlisle*

(Gordon Turner, Lanchester, C. Durham)

The going then became much easier with over 31 miles of downhill running to Carlisle confirming another of Joseph Locke's beliefs; excess fuel used while climbing would be balanced by reduced fuel consumption during the ultimate descent. From Carlisle the situation becomes equally difficult with a ruling gradient of less than 1 in 75 over the 9¾ miles to a summit (at 1,014ft above sea level) between Beattock and Elvanfoot. (Once again, banking engines were employed as standard operating practice.) After the line emerged from the Beattock Hills there was a more or less uninterrupted downhill run through to Glasgow.

The demands of the West Coast main line, with its major summits at Shap and Beattock, were very different from those on the East Coast route and locomotive policy on the two competing systems developed accordingly. On the LNER's East Coast route Sir Nigel Gresley had opportunities, denied to Sir William Stanier, to show the high speed capabilities of his A4 Class streamlined 4-6-2s while Stanier's 4-6-2s had to demonstrate their superior boiler power on a daily basis simply to maintain time over a much more difficult route.

As will be described later, the early LMS was committed to a 'small engine policy' introduced by the Midland Railway, one of its principal constituent companies. Also to be described are changes in LMS senior management; these brought about a review of existing policy followed by the decision to use more powerful locomotives, resulting in the *Royal Scot* 4-6-0s. The Operating Department, previously well-satisfied with what was available, now wanted a locomotive that was not only capable of working on its own and unchanged between Euston and Carlisle but which could continue onwards to Glasgow (in the case of the overnight sleeping car service an additional load, in the form of a heavy 12-wheeled vehicle, was added at Carlisle for preparing and serving

breakfasts). This requirement placed massive demands upon both locomotive and crew. The efficiency of steam locomotives decreases with distance travelled; clinker (from incombustible coal residues) blocks air spaces between the firebars, ash (together with clinker prised away from the firebars by the fireman) fills the ashpan, reducing air flow to the underside of the grate and 'char' (small pieces of unburnt coal and residues) accumulates in the bottom part of the smokebox. In the course of a long journey the amount of accumulated char is sufficient to block lower tubes and this has another adverse effect upon performance.

Under the new policy LMS express passenger locomotives were required to operate a demanding schedule northwards from Euston for some 237 miles when, with ashpan, grate and smokebox rendered less efficient by the accumulated products of combustion, the challenge of climbing over Shap Summit had to be faced. The journey resumed with the same locomotive (and, as mentioned above, often with a heavier load) having to face the demands of the Beattock Hills without any opportunity to empty either ashpan or smokebox. This new policy therefore required locomotives of exceptional power, not only to operate at speed over the relatively easy parts of the route, but to continue working under demanding conditions without steam production becoming impaired by accumulated incombustible residues. (The southbound or 'up' journey was less demanding as the worst hill-climbing was faced at the beginning of the journey instead of at the end.) It was with this requirement in mind that Stanier designed his 4-cylinder 4-6-2s; they were never seriously intended to demonstrate outright maximum speed but were expected to have power in reserve to meet the demands of the West Coast main line and, in this, they succeeded admirably.

As will be seen in a subsequent chapter, the three companies that made the greatest impact, both technically and politically, on the newly formed London Midland & Scottish Railway (LMS) were the Lancashire & Yorkshire (LYR), London & North Western (LNWR) and Midland (MR) Railways. What follows is only a very brief introduction to the locomotive policies of these three companies; anyone wishing for more information should consult the many excellent relevant histories that have been published over the years.

There is little that can be written constructively about the early years of the LYR. E. L. Ahrons, the eminent railway historian, once wrote that in the 1870s the LYR was 'probably the most degenerate railway in the kingdom' and qualified this by stating that it was 'a railway of ugly inconvenient stations, of old broken-down engines and dirty carriages, and of a superlative unpunctuality, to which no pen could do justice'. Later, in anticipation of an early merger between the two companies, the LYR bought a number of new locomotives built by the LNWR at its Crewe Works and this provoked private locomotive builders into setting up the Locomotive Manufacturers' Association. After seeking a judicial review of the legality of one railway manufacturing for another (the Articles of Association of railway companies restrict their trading activities to carrying passengers and goods, although they could build rolling stock for their own use) the Association then succeeded in obtaining a High Court injunction restraining the LNWR from manufacturing for other companies.

With this avenue closed, and with the anticipated merger with the LNWR blocked by Parliament, the LYR appointed William Barton Wright (1828-1915) as its Locomotive Superintendent. He scrapped most existing locomotives, replacing them with a few standard designs, all of which had interchangeable components, and some were built in large numbers. One of his 0-6-0 goods engines, rebuilt by his successor as a saddle tank, was withdrawn by British Railways in 1964, by which time it was 87 years old and the oldest locomotive in routine service (it still survives in preservation). Barton Wright was responsible for much of the layout of the railway's Horwich Works before resigning in 1886. He was replaced by J. A. F. Aspinall (Sir John from 1917) who completed Horwich Works and went on to design several successful standard types including his 2-4-2 radial tank, one of which can be seen at the NRM, York. He was appointed as the LYR's General Manager in 1899 and was replaced by Henry Albert Hoy (1855-1910) who, although a talented electrical engineer, had little success with his steam locomotive designs. His 2-6-2 passenger tank locomotives were failures as was his experiment with corrugated steel stay-less fireboxes built for the railway's 0-8-0 heavy mineral engines. Hoy resigned in 1904 to be replaced by George Hughes (1865-1945) who improved upon his inheritance from Aspinall with designs that benefited from larger boilers and modern superheating based upon the Schmidt principle. While most were successful his *Dreadnought* Class 4-6-0 express passenger engines were initially both unreliable and inefficient but, with lessons learnt, the class was modified and redeemed

A fine portrait of No. 46230 Duchess of Buccleuch *at Carlisle on 19 May 1957. The early BR 'cycling lion' crest is clearly seen*

(Gordon Turner, Lanchester, C. Durham)

No. 46237 City of Bristol *is seen at Birmingham's Snow Hill Station on 28 April 1955 with the 0910 Paddington to Birkenhead express. Around this time the locomotive and other members of the class were on loan to the Western Region*

(T J Edgington Collection)

but the success of Stanier's later 5MT 4-6-0s determined that most would be withdrawn by the LMS. (Only No. 50455 survived long enough to carry its BR number.)

The Liverpool & Manchester Railway, a fundamental component of what became the LNWR, started out with many experimental designs, some of which were both impractical and unreliable. Somewhat later LNWR locomotive policy differed between its Northern Division (with its works at Edge Hill transferring to Crewe in 1843) and the Southern Division, which had completed its works at Wolverton in 1839. In the north, the Grand Junction Railway became dependent upon Stephenson's *Patentee* 2-2-2s (often manufactured under licence) but recurring broken crank axles reduced safety and reliability and increased operating costs. From 1843 onwards they were replaced by small 'Crewe-type' locomotives with outside frames for carrying wheels (often, but incorrectly, referred to as Allan frames); 2-2-2s were used on passenger trains and 2-4-0s for goods traffic. They remained the standard LNWR Northern Division locomotives until 1858 when Francis Trevithick (1812-77) was replaced as locomotive superintendent by John Ramsbottom (1814-97). Edward Bury (1794-1858) held the equivalent position on the Southern Division and used efficient but small 2-2-0s for passenger trains and 0-4-0s, usually for the railway's limited goods traffic but also on fast mail trains; these were designed by his own company but again many were built under licence. Bury resigned in 1847 and was replaced by James Edward McConnell (1815-83) who introduced larger locomotives although some were not too successful.

Ramsbottom became in overall control of

locomotive matters after the divisions were united following McConnell's resignation in 1862. Richard Moon, a director of the LNWR from 1848, was elected as chairman in 1862. Under his stern direction, with economy demanded above everything else, Ramsbottom built a series of neat but lightweight standard locomotives of modest power but low construction and maintenance costs. 943 examples of his DX Class 0-6-0s were built between 1858 and 1872, including those built for the LYR, an all-time record for any British locomotive. Ramsbottom resigned because of declining health in 1871 but recovered sufficiently to hold demanding appointments both with the LYR and Beyer, Peacock & Co, a Manchester-based locomotive builder of international repute. Francis William Webb (1836-1906) was appointed as Ramsbottom's successor and for some years he built and refined Ramsbottom's designs but he was a brilliant and innovative engineer whose positive achievements are often overlooked in the general denigration of his compounds. (With compound expansion, exhaust steam from each high-pressure cylinder is directed to do further work in a low-pressure cylinder, although the full thermodynamic advantages are more complex.) His search for the ideal formula remained elusive although some of his compounds were never the failures that popular history now suggests. The often-repeated *canard* of contra-rotating driving wheels was possible with the slip-eccentric system later adopted for the inside (low-pressure) cylinders of his 3-cylinder compounds, but little contemporary reliable evidence remains of any such outrageous behaviour. Webb's non-compound designs were solidly built and remained in use for many more years with some surviving into Nationalization.

George Whale (1842-1910) assumed control after Webb's retirement in 1903 and scrapped the more troublesome compounds, replacing them with his own 'simple expansion' 4-4-0s and, later, 4-6-0s and 4-4-2Ts. He retained some of Webb's compounds (confirming that they were never as bad as their reputation suggests) and rebuilt others, including the heavy goods 0-8-0s (perhaps the most successful compound design) while adding large numbers of new engines. Charles John Bowen Cooke (1859-1920) took over after Whale's retirement (again on grounds of ill health) in 1909 and was responsible for significant advances in LNWR locomotive technology through adoption of superheating, piston valves and larger cylinders (all inter-related developments) but his major new express passenger type, the 4-cylinder *Claughton* Class 4-6-0s, were designed around earlier technology and could not compete with the superior performance of Churchward's 4-cylinder 4-6-0s, with long travel piston valves, then being built by the GWR. The *Claughtons* looked magnificent but were sadly flawed in terms of reliability, build quality and economy and some were later rebuilt as members of the *Patriot* Class. Bowen Cooke died in 1920, when only 61 years old, and was replaced by Major

H. P. M. Beames (1875-1948) who had little opportunity to make his independent mark before the Grouping of 1923.

The Midland Railway began its corporate existence in 1844 with a very mixed bag of around 110 locomotives, many unsuitable, inherited from its constituent companies but matters began to improve with the appointment of Matthew Kirtley (1813-73) as locomotive superintendent. Unlike the largely self-sufficient LNWR the MR always relied to some extent on private locomotive builders throughout most of its existence and their designs had an early influence on Kirtley but he soon developed the necessary experience and confidence to demand that industry should build to his specifications rather than supply existing types. His designs were robust in construction with double frames and, where appropriate, outside coupling rods; they were never elegant in appearance but they were reliable and worked well, and large numbers of his later locomotives survived to be taken over by the LMS in 1923. He continued with the 2-2-2 arrangement for express passenger trains but changed to 2-4-0s to improve adhesion once train weights increased; he never designed anything larger than 0-6-0 tender engines for goods traffic. As explained in a later chapter, these were all that was required by the railway's successful traffic control system, especially as the MR was prepared

No. 46237 City of Bristol *was transferred temporarily to the Western Region for comparative trials against* King *Class locomotives newly-fitted with high-degree superheating. Here it is seen at Birmingham's Snow Hill Station on 26 April 1955 with the 0910 Paddington to Birkenhead express*

T J Edgington Collection)

No. 46249 City of Sheffield *photographed while on shed at Camden. At the time it was allocated to Crewe North, as confirmed by the famous 5A shed plate*

(Gordon Turner, Lanchester, C. Durham)

for its locomotives to work in tandem (or 'double-headed'). Kirtley died in office when only 60 years old and, at the time of his death, the MR locomotive fleet had increased to around 1,050. He was succeeded by Samuel Waite Johnson (1831-1912) who, in his previous appointment, had been one of many locomotive superintendents employed for relatively brief periods by the Great Eastern Railway.

If Johnson had not been a locomotive engineer then, surely, he would have been a watchmaker or constructor of similar precision instruments, as his engines were beautifully designed and built; moreover, considerable attention was paid to their appearance. He rebuilt many of Kirtley's double-framed locomotives with his own boilers and cabs and the resulting mix of styles (elegance descending into brutality!) had a distinctly individual attraction. Johnson introduced leading bogies on to the MR (his two GER inside-cylinder 4-4-0s were England's first to have this arrangement but Britain's first were designed for Scotland's North British Railway by Thomas Wheatley, born at Micklefield, near Leeds) and he used inside-framed 4-4-0s for principal passenger trains until 1887 when a combination of factors resulted in a renaissance of the British 'single'. Johnson then introduced his celebrated 4-2-2s, an elegant design that can still be admired at the NRM, York but continued with the 0-6-0 arrangement for goods and local passenger trains although, in 1901, he broke the tradition of slow, incremental power increases when the first MR 3-cylinder compound appeared.

For many years Webb persevered with a 3-cylinder arrangement in which outside high-pressure cylinders exhausted into a single, very large, low-pressure cylinder positioned between the frames. An alternative system, first introduced by the French engineer, Edouard Sauvage, used a central single high-pressure cylinder exhausting into two outside low-pressure cylinders of similar (but not identical) dimensions and, with all pistons having similar diameters (and, more, importantly, similar weights) locomotives were better balanced. This idea was developed by Walter Mackerzie Smith (1842-1906) who was the North Eastern Railway's chief draughtsman under Wilson Worsdell, the latter giving Smith permission to rebuild NER 4-4-0 No. 1619 as a 3-cylinder compound. Smith retained his friendship with Johnson from their early days on the Edinburgh & Glasgow Railway and, resulting from an exchange of ideas, no doubt encouraged by Worsdell, Johnson built some 4-4-0 compounds based on the Smith/Sauvage system for the MR. The first Midland *Compound* No. 1000 is preserved at the NRM, York in the condition following its rebuilding in 1914. Johnson retired at the end of 1903 to be replaced by Richard Mountford Deeley (1855-1944) whose few years as Locomotive Superintendent (he resigned in 1909) were marred by MR internecine warfare. His most memorable contribution was his elegant redesign of the *Compounds* that simplified (mechanically and aesthetically) Johnson's florid and excessively complex creation. Although only 45 were built by the MR many more were to follow under the auspices of the early LMS, which added 195 similar but not identical locomotives between 1924 and 1932.

Henry Fowler, later Sir Henry, KBE, DSc (1870-1938) assumed control of MR locomotive matters in 1909 but it must be questioned whether he was ever committed to the job; he was a scientist of international repute whose versatility was confirmed through his appointments as Director of Production to the Ministry of Munitions in 1915, Assistant Director General of Aircraft Production in 1917 and President of the Institute of Automobile Engineers in 1920. His MR locomotive designs were limited to a large-boilered superheated 0-6-0 (the 4F Class, with 772 built up to 1941) which was let down by poor front-end design and undersized (but standard) axlebox bearings and the single 0-10-0 *Lickey Banker*, originally MR No. 2290 and withdrawn by BR as No. 58100 in 1956. This locomotive, known unofficially as either *Big Bertha* or *Big Emma*, was much lauded by enthusiasts mightily impressed by its sight and sound in action; such impressions were, unfortunately, the result of serious thermodynamic inefficiency.

After the 1923 Grouping George Hughes, previously of the LYR, became the new LMS Chief Mechanical Engineer and under his direction the LMS 2-6-0s (referred to unofficially as *Crabs*) were designed at the former LYR offices at Horwich. Differences of opinion within the new order resulted in his resignation in 1925 and the appointment of Sir Henry Fowler as his successor. Fowler's 'contributions' to the LMS included a slightly modified version of the 4-4-0 Compound, a development of Johnson's shunting 0-6-0T first introduced in 1874, a slightly revised 4-4-0 with built-in front-end problems, an 0-8-0 heavy goods engine with an improved front-end but

inadequate bearings, a 2-6-2T that performed poorly, being underpowered and overweight and a successful 2-6-4T that was designed at Horwich without MR constraints. This efficient design was later developed into standard types by William Stanier (for the LMS) and Robin Riddles (for British Railways). Other designs were attributed to Fowler, including the LMS Beyer-Garratt type 2-6-6-2 mineral engines, but these owed more to the Operating Department whose specification once again included inadequate standard axlebox bearings.

As will be shown there was to be a total reorganization of LMS senior management and within this was included the appointment of Sir Josiah Charles Stamp (1880-1941) whose massive influence on the LMS is described in a later chapter. The above notes emphasize that in its early years the LMS continued to embrace the Midland Railway's 'small engine' policy and while some large express passenger designs were inherited from both the LNWR (the *Claughton* Class 4-6-0s) and LYR (the 4-6-0 *Dreadnoughts*) neither demonstrated the advanced technical features developed by the GWR under Churchward that were being employed by engineers on other railways. The LMS was content to build *Midland Compound* 4-4-0s (with a 4P power rating) and to use them in tandem whenever necessary (which was quite often) irrespective of higher manpower, operating and maintenance costs. Collett's GWR *Castle* Class 4-6-0s and Gresley's A3 Class 4-6-2s both had power ratings of 7P and, other than under exceptional conditions, they worked their trains unaided. It was apparent to all 'railway watchers' at the time that the LMS was digging itself into an operating hole and that considerable ingenuity, effort and, above all, investment would be required before it could escape.

An early photograph of LMS No. 6221 Queen Elizabeth, *the second 'blue streamliner' to be completed. This view emphasises the distance between chimney and bufferbeam and puts into proper perspective some of the problems encountered in fabricating* Duchess of Hamilton's *streamlined smokebox doors without the benefit of working drawings*

(Gresley Society)

Britain's railways emerged from the Great War of 1914-18 in a very run-down condition because of sacrifices made (individually and corporately) for the war effort in terms of manpower, materials and equipment; the situation was exacerbated by strict Government controls over passenger fares and goods tariffs during a period of soaring operating costs. Post-war there were many calls for nationalization from all political parties (Winston Churchill supported this option) but an effectively bankrupt nation was unable to compensate shareholders who had invested in the railway companies. After much debate a 'grouping' into four large geographical groups was accepted as a working compromise and the resulting arrangements were embodied in the Railways Act of 1921, which received Royal Assent on 19 August 1921. Under this Act four new large railway companies, the London, Midland & Scottish (LMS), London & North Eastern (LNER), Great Western (GWR) and Southern (SR) Railways came into existence on 1 January 1923 although, for various legal reasons, some companies were not included until 1 July 1923. Under the Act all major pre-grouping railways became 'constituents' and were 'amalgamated' into the larger group with the right to appoint Directors while smaller companies were classed as 'subsidiaries' and were 'absorbed'. (Prior to the 1921 Act the Government had opposed most proposed amalgamations as it considered that any resultant monopoly would be prejudicial to public interest!)

The LMS had eight constituent companies, the London & North Western (LNWR), Midland (MR), Lancashire & Yorkshire (LYR), North Staffordshire (NSR), Furness (FR), Caledonian (CR), Glasgow & South Western (GSWR) and Highland (HR) Railways, and some twenty-seven subsidiaries but only five of these owned their own locomotives. The NSR and FR were too small to exert much influence and, as Scottish companies distanced themselves by their opposition to the grouping, the resulting and entirely predictable struggle for supremacy within the LMS was between the LNWR (with its base at Crewe), the LYR (based at Horwich) and the MR (with its works at Derby). To increase their joint impact the LNWR and LYR arranged a preliminary amalgamation in January 1922 and, because of their seniority (in terms of the number of years in post) the LYR's General Manager (Arthur Watson) and Chief Mechanical Engineer (George Hughes) were appointed to similar positions within the enlarged LNWR. The latter was a talented and innovative locomotive engineer who, among other successful developments, had made a significant contribution to the adoption of superheating.

Both men were sufficiently senior to retain their positions within the newly-created LMS but the battle was far from won as Sir Guy Granet, a former MR General Manager and later Director, became one of two LMS Deputy Chairmen and was appointed as Chairman within a year. Many senior staff appointments were then 'within his

Duchess of Hamilton powers 'The Limited Edition' out of York Station on 10 May 1980, making its first run after restoration to main line working condition
(Roger Bastin)

Until William Stanier's arrival in 1932, the LMS continued building 3-cylinder compound 4-4-0s for main line express passenger traffic which were based upon a Midland Railway design dating back to 1902. The prototype, MR No. 1000, is now preserved at the NRM and is seen here leaving York on 28 September 1983 with a special charter to Rochdale   *(NRM Collection)*

gift' including those of General Superintendent and Superintendent of Motive Power and these posts were awarded to J. H. Follows and J. E. Anderson respectively, both former MR senior officers. These appointments meant that key MR policies were perpetuated by the LMS, including the effective subordination of the CME's authority by the Motive Power Superintendent and continued expansion of the MR's centralized traffic control system.

In the early years of the 20th century the MR's mineral traffic developed to the extent that the railway was unable to cope efficiently. Goods trains, dispatched on schedule, were often diverted into a succession of sidings to allow the unimpeded passage of passenger trains and the resulting delays had many undesirable consequences. They were unacceptable to the railway, which had to provide fuel, water and staff for locomotives that remained in steam despite being stationary for much of the day, and to customers who had little idea as to when their goods might arrive. Locomotive crews were especially disadvantaged as they often worked exceptionally long hours, often in extremely uncomfortable conditions. (20,000 such cases

were recorded in 1907 prior to introduction of the traffic control system but within four years there were no further instances, thereby providing an invaluable performance indicator to the system's effectiveness.)

The traffic control system was pioneered by J. H. Follows, then Traffic Inspector for the Derby District and was first tried experimentally at Masborough near Sheffield; it was so successful that it was extended to cover the whole Midland Railway network under the direction of Cecil Paget, then General Superintendent. Large diagrams were prepared to show all available railway facilities within each district with designated fast and slow lines, alternative routes, refuge sidings and information vital when re-routing trains such as the precise location of water troughs and cranes. The progress of trains throughout some 42 sections was reported by telephone to a Central Control at Derby but District Controllers had ultimate responsibility for traffic within their area. The system had serious repercussions for the Locomotive Department, the first of which seemed entirely cosmetic. The MR followed American practice and displayed each locomotive's number in large characters either on the tender or tank side, simplifying the job of signalmen who were now required to identify and report the passage of each train. (Prior to the system's introduction, standard safety procedures required signalmen to 'accept' trains and then 'offer' them to the next signal box without having to monitor working timetable efficiency.) The second impact of the system established loads for each locomotive class not only within each section but for different weather conditions; the system was so rigid that, should the load exceed the stipulated figure by as little as one axle then a second locomotive had to be provided.

The system worked and the punctuality achieved by the MR became a yardstick against which other railways were measured and, initially, most failed to achieve the same high standard. There was, however, a price to pay. The task of setting up the system was considerable and there was neither time, will nor opportunity to implement regular revisions. The MR was never short of locomotives so, whenever loads exceeded the arbitrary stated limit, pilot engines were readily available and the motive power department saw nothing wrong with the situation. Whenever new locomotives were required the locomotive department had to produce 'more of the same' simply for operating convenience and, despite significant advances being made elsewhere in Britain, Derby had no incentive to follow and MR locomotive development became static. However, as years went by, train loads increased inexorably, especially with heavier modern passenger bogie stock and, it must be added, many contributions to passenger comfort were initiated by the MR, most resulting in an increased tare weight per passenger. Nevertheless the railway became known as a 'small engine line' always prepared to use two small locomotives when, on other railways, one larger and more powerful engine would suffice. In reality it had painted itself into a corner. Because of the limited capacity

of its main lines it could not divide its traffic into a larger number of separate smaller trains, each within the capacity of a single locomotive, it could not abandon the traffic control system, on which its continued prosperity depended; nor could it insist that its locomotives should perform feats of haulage beyond their intended design limits. Even at this stage it seemed obvious that larger engines were necessary but this message failed to receive official approval.

The result was not only Derby's continued production of many more small engines but in the retention of large numbers of older locomotives for use as pilots on double-headed trains. At the time of grouping the MR contributed 2,925 steam locomotives to the LMS and of these 288 were passenger types considered obsolete on the main lines of other British railways (245 Kirtley and Johnson 2-4-0s and 43 Johnson 4-2-2s) and another 471 were old Kirtley double-framed goods engines. While these figures suggest that one quarter of the MR's locomotive stock was used only for piloting, the true situation was even worse as there were many occasions when quite modern engines were used in tandem.

With Sir Guy Granet as the LMS Chairman and Follows and Anderson as his able lieutenants, to be joined in 1925 by Sir Henry Fowler, the former CME of the MR (whose LMS appointment resulted from George Hughes' resignation) the MR's stranglehold was complete. The MR's traffic control system was expanded to include the new, enlarged LMS network (which, in itself, was no bad thing) but the consequent small engine policy was also imposed and this, without doubt, was a disaster as the busy West Coast main line out of Euston could not readily be adapted for handling larger numbers of light, single-engine trains.

A fine portrait of No. 6224 Princess Alexandra *soon after de-streamlining, retaining the sloping smokebox top. The livery at the time was gloss black with 'straw' lining*

(Gresley Society)

Under Fowler's direction the LMS built 575 0-6-0s (of a type first introduced in 1911 but, even then, it was little more than a superheated version of a much older design) and 138 two-cylinder 4-4-0s (to which the same reservations apply). Heavy goods traffic was handled by 175 0-8-0s, introduced in 1929 as a 'Midlandised' version of Webb's celebrated LNWR design that first appeared in 1892 (albeit as a compound) and, for its principal main line expresses, the LMS built 195 three-cylinder compound 4-4-0s from 1924 onwards, perpetuating a design that first appeared on the MR in 1902. The LMS did have 245 modern, powerful mixed-traffic engines that were built between 1926 and 1932. These were the 5P5F, later 5F, *Crab* 2-6-0s, designed largely by Hughes at Horwich prior to his resignation. Fowler's involvement in the design of the locomotive proper was minimal but he insisted upon adoption of the standard MR tender which was eighteen inches narrower than the locomotives' footplates, creating a potentially lethal hazard for the crew.

Elsewhere, however, things were very different. On the GWR Churchward introduced his two-cylinder *Saint* Class 4-6-0s for express passenger services in 1902 and, in 1906, they were followed by his four-cylinder *Star* Class 4-6-0s, later to be further developed under Collett into the *Castle* Class of 1923 and the *King* Class of 1927. Heavy freight was handled by the 2800 Class 2-8-0s (this wheel arrangement being considered superior to the 0-8-0s as it caused less track and tyre wear while reducing strain on locomotive frames and bearings), with 168 examples being constructed. On the SR Maunsell developed Urie's earlier express passenger 4-6-0s into the *King Arthur* Class of 1925 to be followed by his four-cylinder *Lord Nelson* Class 4-6-0s of 1926. Gresley's progress on the LNER was even more dramatic. His GNR three-cylinder 4-6-2s, introduced in 1922 were developed further with revised valve gear and higher operating pressure into the A3 Class of 1927 and, somewhat later, into the streamlined A4s of 1935. In 1934 he introduced 2-8-2 express passenger locomotives for services between Edinburgh and Aberdeen and, after building 20 two-cylinder 2-8-0s for the GNR, he used three cylinders on what became the LNER's standard heavy goods 2-8-0s built from 1921 onwards. (His intention to build many

No. 46220 Coronation, *seen at Glasgow (Polmadie) on 26 June 1957. As the first of the 'blue streamliners' it was based at Polmadie (shed No. 66A) for much of its life*   (Gordon Turner, Lanchester, C. Durham)

more was frustrated by the LNER's post-war purchase of large numbers of surplus ROD 2-8-0s based upon Robinson's Great Central Railway design.)

All of this confirmed that the LMS was years behind the other three post-grouping companies in terms of technical development and, with increasing competition for traffic to the north (not only from railway companies, as both road and air transport were emerging as serious alternatives), there was little room for complacency. Fortunately a significant appointment was made in January 1926 when, at the instigation of Sir Guy Granet, Sir Josiah Stamp was recruited as the President of the Executive. The effects of his timely appointment are described in the following chapter.

The Impact of Sir Josiah (later Lord) Stamp

In terms of turnover and asset value the LMS was one of the world's largest companies owned by private and corporate investors and its management was both complex and onerous. Sir Guy Granet recognized the difficulties faced by a single General Manager and introduced an American-style Executive with a President and four Vice-Presidents, each with the authority of a General Manager within their sphere of responsibility. The Executive was supported by three others, including the Company Secretary and Chief Legal Advisor and, while there was little doubt concerning initial Vice-Presidential appointments (all coming from within the railway industry) Sir Guy Granet needed someone with wider experience and different expertise as President, his choice falling upon Sir Josiah Charles Stamp.

Josiah Stamp was born in Kilburn, London on 21 June 1880 as the third of seven children. His father had managed the railway bookstall at Wigan before moving to London, where he opened a provisions shop. Josiah left school when aged fifteen and, after passing the Civil Service entrance examination, started work as an Inland Revenue clerk. His studies during this time were rewarded by a first-class honours degree to be followed by a Doctor of Science degree a few years later. Natural ability coupled with inexhaustible energy resulted in rapid promotion and he became Assistant Secretary to the Board of Inland Revenue by the age of 36 and was already recognized as one of Britain's foremost economists. He left the Civil Service in 1919 to become both Secretary and Director of Nobel Industries Ltd (later expanded into Imperial Chemical Industries) and was awarded a KBE in 1920. In January 1926 he became the first President of the LMS Executive and in March 1927, after retirement of the General Manager, Burgess, all of the latter's residual responsibilities were transferred to Stamp. Sir Guy Granet retired in October 1927 and Stamp replaced him as Chairman with the LMS becoming his principal business activity from 1931 onwards. Granet later observed that 'I can only say that I have never seen a railway manager or chairman give up so many hours to the daily service of his company' and he was known to work exceptionally long hours on six days each week, including time spent when travelling on the company's business in his 'austerely comfortable' carriage with its bed and bathroom. On the seventh day he could often be found teaching in Sunday school.

Without railway managerial experience Stamp could ask meaningful questions without anyone expecting him to know that 'things have always been done this way'. His questions must have included 'why do LMS trains require two engines while those on other railways need only one?' and he must have been concerned by the answers. As an economist he needed improved utilization and availability of locomotives, greater standardization, fewer spares and, above all, elimination of double-heading, especially whenever four men were paid for work that could readily be done by two. There was an early response to his initiatives when GWR No. 5000 *Launceston Castle* arrived on the LMS in September 1926 (without prior knowledge of the CME!) and demonstrated precisely what could be

Duchess of Hamilton *at Stainforth (Sheriff Brow), near the southern end of the Settle & Carlisle line, on 19 October 1983* (Roger Bastin)

On 5 November 1983 Duchess of Hamilton *heads the 'Cumbrian Mountain Express' in Carlisle Station. Note the NRM's support coach immediately behind the locomotive*

(Roger Bastin)

expected from a single modern multi-cylinder locomotive, first working between Euston and Crewe and then over the more difficult road to Carlisle.

The result was that J. E. Anderson, the LMS Superintendent of Motive Power and previously an unequivocal proponent of Derby's small engine policy, requested that between twenty and fifty *Castle* Class locomotives be ordered but was frustrated by the GWR's failure to oblige. (The GWR was unable to comply, even had it so wished, as a legal injunction, referred to earlier, prevented railway companies from manufacturing locomotives for sale to others unless statutorily authorized.) The LMS then requested drawings of Collett's *Castle* Class but, while Swindon was prepared to demonstrate what could be done, it was less willing to expose how it had been achieved. At the LMS's request, Richard Maunsell, the SR's CME, forwarded drawings of his new four-cylinder *Lord Nelson* Class 4-6-0s and these, together with existing LMS drawings and patterns, were sent to the North British Locomotive Company, which had been awarded a design-and-build contract for a new LMS express passenger 4-6-0 design. All negotiations took place without the CME, Sir Henry Fowler, becoming involved and his ongoing development of a four-cylinder compound 4-6-2 was summarily cancelled. The new three-cylinder 4-6-0s became the *Royal Scots* and, although immediately effective, they became less reliable and economic with time and as problems emerged.

It was during 1927 that the LMS ordered its Beyer-Garratt articulated 2-6-6-2 locomotives for heavy mineral

traffic but, once again, specifications were drawn up by the Superintendent of Motive Power without reference to the CME. Legitimate objections raised by Beyer, Peacock & Co, the builders, were over-ruled in favour of a flawed hybrid incorporating shortcomings such as standard MR axlebox bearings which, while adequate for the light work required under the traffic control system, were unequal to the demands of heavier trains. Sir Henry Fowler's position became untenable and, in 1930 when aged 60, he was moved sideways to a newly-created executive position as Assistant to the Vice-President for Works (Research and Development). This appointment was more appropriate to his qualifications and interests and he went on to establish the LMS Scientific Research Laboratory which opened at Derby in 1935 and was further developed by British Railways.

With Fowler transferred there was an opportunity to appoint a dynamic CME prepared to insist upon technological development and to challenge the dead hand of the Motive Power Department but the appointment of Ernest John Hutchings Lemon came as an anti-climax. Lemon was a talented production engineer (he became Director General of Aircraft Production during World War Two and was knighted for his achievements; later he was involved in planning post-war railways) but two things counted against him. Firstly, most of his expertise was gained not with locomotives but within the Carriage & Wagon department and, secondly, he was a 'dyed in the wool' Midland Railway man who was unlikely to bring peace to the warring tribes at Crewe and Horwich

Already relegated to more mundane duties, No. 46220 Coronation *works a parcels train through Coventry*   (*T J Edgington Collection*)

(although Derby would have been well satisfied with his appointment!). The worst fears of 'LMS watchers' were realised when the first (but, fortunately, the only) locomotive design appeared during Lemon's period of office. The Motive Power Department requested ten locomotives for working suburban 'push-pull' motor trains and Lemon duly obliged with 0-4-4Ts that were slightly modified and updated versions of Samuel Johnson's 1875 locomotives which were based upon his even earlier designs for the GER. It seemed to be another case of 'The Mixture, As Before'!

Some maintain that Lemon's was intended as a long-term appointment but the more widely accepted view is that he was called upon to fill the interregnum between Fowler and A. N. Other, providing time for the latter to be identified and his appointment confirmed. J. H. Follows was in declining health and took premature retirement from his position as Vice-President, Railway Traffic, Operating & Commercial in 1932 to be replaced by Lemon. Many now accept that this move was planned in advance as part of an overall strategy, especially as Lemon's 'alternative' contributions to the continued prosperity of the LMS were considerable. His departure left the CME's post vacant, with two internal applicants, both with excellent credentials, Major H. M. P. Beames CBE, the Deputy CME under Lemon and someone immersed in the LNWR Crewe philosophy and S. J. Symes, the CME's Personal Assistant and an engineer adhering to the MR's way of doing things. With both representing opposing factions within the LMS, the appointment of either would have added a further undesirable element to an already worrying internecine situation. Stamp observed that had the LNWR candidate been appointed there would have been great rejoicing at Crewe with dancing in the park but, if the decision had been in favour of the MR man, Crewe would have been in revolt! It became obvious that the new incumbent should have feet in neither camp but should

possess the experience, expertise and authority necessary to gain immediate respect and co-operation from all concerned.

Before this could be achieved there was a further personality to be considered. Sir Harold Hartley had been appointed as the new Vice-President for Works & Ancillary Services following the death in March 1929 (at the age of 45) of Robert Whyte Reid CBE, who was the son of W. P. Reid CBE, formerly Locomotive Superintendent of the North British Railway. After Reid's untimely death some (no doubt including Sir Henry Fowler) considered that they had a valid claim for Vice Presidential status but Sir Josiah Stamp insisted upon another 'non-railway' appointment. Sir Harold Hartley was a distinguished scientist and a previous Director of Chemical Warfare during the Great War (long before the current but globally incomplete ban on such activities) and a man whose 'abounding energy' matched that of Sir Josiah himself. Under direction from Sir Josiah Stamp, Sir Harold Hartley took 'soundings' and decided that the new occupant of the post of LMS CME should be William Arthur Stanier, later to be recognized as one of the giants among later locomotive engineers.

The significant contribution made by William Arthur Stanier (knighted in 1943 and elected as a Fellow of the Royal Society in 1944) is described in succeeding chapters. Before detailing these there is one final irony to be recorded concerning Sir Josiah Stamp. After the Great War he was the British representative on the 'Dawes Committee', the recommendations of which formed the basis of Germany's State Railway (Deutsche Reichsbahn) that came into existence in October 1924 through unification of the country's railways. Dawes, the chairman, once remarked that Stamp's contribution was of such magnitude that the resulting organizational structure should have been named 'the Stamp Plan'. Subsequently he played a key role in fostering Anglo-German relationships in matters such as

An immaculate Princess Royal Class *No. 6210* Lady Patricia *recently turned out in postwar lined black livery*   *(Gresley Society)*

An interesting view of No. 6224 Princess Alexandra *showing external details of the tender coal pusher with the side panels of the de-streamlined tender standing proud of the back plate*   *(Gresley Society)*

finance and transport. In 1938 he was elevated to the peerage as Baron Stamp of Shortlands and later, in 1940, he was offered, but declined, the post of Chancellor of the Exchequer in the wartime coalition government. He, his wife and son were killed on the night of 16/17th April 1941, all victims of a German air raid over London.

Sir William Wood, his successor, said of him that 'he created the LMS as a single and closely integrated machine, with maximum efficiency at minimum cost'.

Others, including LMS passengers on the less-favoured secondary routes, considered his economies unacceptable and he was sometimes likened to a tax inspector who, although usually approachable, could be utterly ruthless whenever necessary. However, there is no doubt that Josiah Stamp was responsible not only for bringing William Stanier to the LMS but also for creating the right financial conditions for Stanier's 'mighty restocking' of the railway and, indirectly, for the appearance of the *Coronation* Class.

Appointment of William (later Sir William) Arthur Stanier

William Arthur Stanier was born on the 27th May 1876 at Swindon, Wiltshire, where his father was the Stores Superintendent under William Dean at the GWR's Swindon Works. (Coincidentally Herbert Nigel Gresley was born just a few weeks later on the 19th June and, while their careers were very different, both became accepted as the finest British locomotive engineers in the post-Churchward era.) Stanier's father had been Dean's chief clerk at Wolverhampton and had moved to Swindon on the latter's appointment as Chief Assistant to Joseph Armstrong. Armstrong died in 1877, when Dean became the Locomotive, Carriage & Wagon Superintendent, and continued to be supported by Stanier (senior), who introduced mechanical and chemical testing of bought-in materials (at first working in his own kitchen) as well as inaugurating technical education for Swindon apprentices at the Mechanics Institute.

From an early age William Stanier decided upon a career in engineering and, perhaps as a consequence, his academic achievements at Wycliffe College, Stonehouse, Gloucestershire, were never outstanding. (The feeling is that his end-of-term reports might have been endorsed 'could do better'!) He started working for the GWR as an office boy in January 1892 and began his formal apprenticeship on reaching sixteen years of age. May 1892 was a memorable month for the GWR as, in one dramatic weekend of carefully co-ordinated activity, remaining broad gauge lines were converted to standard gauge. It should not be thought that the long-standing association between Dean and Stanier (senior) was of advantage to the young William as there were many apprentices within Swindon Works; the great man could not be expected to know them all, especially as his health was in decline.

From 1894 the GWR rebuilt four experimental 2-4-0s into *Armstrong* Class 4-4-0s and these were, arguably, the most visually attractive engines ever built to this wheel arrangement. William Stanier was involved in the reconstruction of one, No. 14 (later No. 4170 *Charles Saunders*), and his first footplate experiences also came during his apprenticeship when he was required to accompany these engines, and the celebrated *Dean Single* 4-2-2s, on their post-works trial runs. On completion of his five-year apprenticeship in 1897 Stanier's Swindon experience expanded through working in the pattern shop, drawing office (with special involvement in carriage and wagon development) and the locomotive, experimental and structure sections and, in December 1899, he was appointed as Inspector of Materials. Running shed experience then followed when, as a mechanical (or technical) inspector working under the Divisional Locomotive Superintendent at Swindon, Stanier managed the work of all fitters and boilermakers responsible for maintaining around one hundred locomotives at Swindon together with those at dependent sheds including

LMS No. 6233 Duchess of Sunderland, *the only one of three preserved members of the Duchess Class to be in main line working order, arrives at York's No. 5 Platform on June 9th 2007*

(Graham Dudley)

On 25 June 1957 Duchess of Hamilton *was photographed north of Penrith with the 1615 down 'Caledonian' from Euston, around two weeks after the service was* *inaugurated*

(*J M Chamney*)

Gloucester, Severn & Wye, Oxford, Reading, Trowbridge and Weymouth. This was a key appointment as, in addition to preparing locomotives for their daily scheduled work, Swindon shed was responsible for new locomotives during their running-in period. In the years prior to and immediately following Dean's retirement Churchward introduced a number of new designs (many experimental) and Stanier would have been involved as they entered traffic.

Although only 27 years old, Stanier was considered sufficiently experienced to take charge of the London Division in 1903 during the temporary absence of John Armstrong, the Divisional Locomotive, Carriage & Wagon Superintendent based at Westbourne Park. Following Armstrong's return from America Stanier spent further months at Swindon before returning to the London Division in 1904, this time as Armstrong's assistant. This was a dramatic time. Churchward was continuing his search for the locomotive types best suited for GWR service and development depended upon receiving full and accurate reports from senior running shed staff personnel while, at the same time, the same staff were transferring work from the restricted former broad-gauge shed at Westbourne Park to the new round house complex at Old Oak Common.

It was here that Stanier became involved in an event that probably confirmed his status as someone marked out for advancement within the GWR management structure. Locomotive engineers worldwide were impressed by the de Glehn/du Bousquet compound 4-4-2s introduced on the French Nord Railway and many visited France to inspect them at work. Churchward went even better and received authority to buy one directly from the builders, the Société Alsacienne des Constructions Méchaniques, Belfort, and this was delivered in 1903 as No. 102 *La France*. Two slightly larger versions, based upon those built for the Paris-Orleans Railway, were delivered in 1905 to become GWR Nos. 103 *President* and 104 *Alliance*, the Pennsylvania Railroad also buying a similar locomotive at the same time. In order to achieve a level playing field for a series of comparative trials, Churchward converted one of his earliest *Saint* Class 2-cylinder 4-6-0s (No. 171 *Albion*) into the 4-4-2 arrangement before building others from new as 4-4-2s. Most were used on the West Country main line from Paddington and were based at Old Oak Common from where Stanier had the unenviable responsibility of informing Swindon that the new 4-4-2s steamed badly when compared with either the 4-6-0s or the converted No. 171. He was summoned to Churchward's office to face interrogation. Fortunately Stanier went well prepared; after studying the drawings he decided that the new straight-bottomed ashpan restricted air flow to the fire grate. Churchward agreed, the engines were modified, good steaming was restored and, without doubt, Stanier's career benefited.

In April 1906 Stanier was back at Swindon as Assistant to the Locomotive Works Manager but later the same year he became Divisional Locomotive Superintendent at Swindon, where, until late 1912, it was his responsibility to oversee the running-in of all locomotives, newly-built or overhauled, emerging from Swindon Works. Many of Churchward's standard types appeared during this period together with the 'one-off' 4-6-2 No. 111 *The Great Bear* (the GWR's only Pacific) as did all of Churchward's superheating experiments and developments.

Stanier's days in the running department ended in December 1912. H. C. King, the Locomotive Works Manager at Swindon since 1902, was appointed as Assistant to the Chief Mechanical Engineer and C. B. Collett, his Assistant during the same period, was promoted to Works Manager. Stanier then became the Assistant Works Manager, a post that he retained until 1920. It was a time of great difficulties as during the Great War, Swindon, like most other locomotive works, devoted much capacity to armament production. The scale of locomotive construction was reduced but repairs had to continue; the railways' contribution to the war effort was vital but their efforts were frustrated by acute manpower and material shortages. (Railway work was considered important enough to gain exemption from military service but, prior to compulsory conscription, large numbers of railwaymen volunteered to 'join the Colours'.)

Prior to William Dean's retirement in 1902 the GWR ensured a smooth transition from the retiring CME to his successor by appointing Churchward as Dean's Chief Assistant and, with Churchward due to retire in December

1921, GWR management followed a similar procedure, appointing Collett as Deputy CME late in 1919. This gave Stanier promotion to Locomotive Works Manager in 1920 but only until 1922, when he became the Works Assistant to the Chief Mechanical Engineer who, by now, was Charles Benjamin Collett OBE. It was obvious to Stanier that time was against him. Collett was his senior by only five years and, even if he retired at sixty-five, the CME's post would not become vacant until 1936, by which time Stanier might have been considered too old for promotion. (In the event Collett's retirement was deferred until 1941; many now believe that he should have left earlier while his previously excellent reputation remained intact.)

Late in 1927, however, Stanier was to receive considerable media attention (by the conservative standards of the day) but the explanation is a little complex. Churchward intended that the GWR's standard express locomotives should be 2-cylinder 4-6-0s but the smooth running of the French 4-cylinder compound 4-4-2s with their divided drive persuaded him otherwise and his first 4-cylinder (non-compound) *Star* Class 4-6-0 appeared in 1906. These were developed by Collett into the celebrated *Castle* Class introduced in 1923 which were followed in 1927 by the heavier *King* Class. The *Kings* were less of an operational requirement and more of a public relations exercise as, in terms only of nominal tractive effort, they became Britain's most powerful passenger locomotives. The American Baltimore & Ohio Railroad wished to celebrate its centenary in 1927 with a pageant similar to that organized in 1925 for the Stockton & Darlington Centenary event and it was agreed that the GWR should be represented by its most powerful and prestigious

A grimy No. 46233 Duchess of Sutherland *(now, happily, also preserved) was photographed at Birmingham's New Street Station on 17 February 1962 with the 0845 Euston to Wolverhampton express*

(*T J Edgington Collection*)

No. 46244 King George VI, *in a commendably clean condition, arrives at Euston in May 1964 with an up 'Shamrock' express. The locomotive was withdrawn in September 1964*

(T J Edgington Collection)

locomotive. Names for the new class had not been decided (*Cathedral* names were being considered) but the opportunity to display an engine in the USA resulted in the patriotic decision to name them after British Kings, the first becoming No. 6000 *King George V*. In what was a precedent for an event some twelve years later, No. 6000 was shipped to Baltimore, accompanied by Driver Young, Fireman Pearce, Fitters Williams and Dando and with Stanier in overall control. *King George V* made a most favourable impression, and not only as a static exhibit, as a 272-mile demonstration run with a train of seven heavy-weight American carriages (with a tare weight of $543^1/2$ tons) was arranged immediately after the exhibition closed. Despite an unfamiliar route (a B&O pilotman was on the footplate), different signals, unsuitable coal and a load in excess of the GWR's heaviest peacetime trains, the engine put up an excellent performance, a tribute to its design, construction, preparation and handling on the day.

Back at Swindon Stanier became Collett's Principal Assistant and, with no further promotion possible within the GWR he was able to concentrate on his principal tasks, which included further development of Swindon's workshop procedures and extending the interval between each locomotive's visits to works for major repairs. The trial which took place over the LMS main line in September 1926 with GWR No. 5000 *Launceston Castle* convinced the LMS Board that its own locomotives were inferior to those of the GWR and this, no doubt, was of considerable satisfaction to those at Swindon but there is no evidence to suggest that the LMS intended to recruit any senior GWR personnel at this time.

By his own account Stanier was mystified to receive an invitation to have lunch at the *Athenaeum* Club with E. J. H. Lemon, ostensibly to discuss water softening as, while he had experience of the subject, so did the LMS, through its Scottish constituent companies. They were joined by Sir Harold Hartley, the LMS Vice-President for Works & Ancillary Services. Later there came a second invitation, this time for lunch at the *Travellers* Club with Sir Harold Hartley when the subject for discussion was Stanier's possible transfer to the LMS CME post. Stanier reported this proposal to Collett and requested that it be brought to the attention of the GWR General Manager, when it was confirmed that as Collett would not be taking early retirement there was little likelihood of Stanier becoming GWR's next CME. Correspondence between Sir Josiah Stamp and Viscount Churchill, the GWR Chairman, completed the formal arrangements that allowed William Stanier to resign from the GWR to take up his new appointment with the LMS effective from 1 January 1932.

Sir Harold Hartley later reported that 'after looking over the possible field when Lemon became a Vice-President, I decided that Stanier was the man to get our locomotive programme straightened out. The number of different types we had inherited was appalling. I had no second string, so I went ahead on my own with Stamp's blessing. I knew something of the Churchward tradition.' And so it was that William Stanier abandoned the certainties of life at Swindon to face unknown difficulties on the LMS. He could not have known their precise nature in advance but, as a railway professional, he would have realized that many serious problems awaited his arrival.

An official works portrait of newly completed No. 6200 The Princess Royal. *Note the vacuum pump operated from the left crosshead, the original domeless boiler (but with top feed) and the standard small-capacity MR tender*
(Gresley Society)

The *Royal Scot* 4-6-0s, with their ability to handle up to 420-ton express passenger trains between London (Euston) and Carlisle, had revolutionized the LMS Operating Department's thinking and it now requested a locomotive capable of working 500-ton loads unaided from London to Glasgow. This was Stanier's first objective after taking over the responsibilities of the Locomotive Department and it was to the credit of everyone involved that 4-6-2 No. 6200 (later *The Princess Royal*) appeared from Crewe Works on 1st July 1933, just eighteen months after his appointment. Critics sometimes regard this as a 4-6-2 version of the GWR's *King* Class 4-6-0 but, while many dimensions were common to both designs, Stanier's independence was already apparent.

The four cylinders were identical to those of the *King* Class (16¼in-diameter and 28in-stroke) and boiler pressure at 250 pounds per square inch (psi) was the same but the tapered boiler barrel had a larger diameter and was more than four feet longer. Piston valves on both inside and outside cylinders were actuated by four separate sets of Walschaert motion unlike GWR 4-6-0s, where inside motion was used to drive outside cylinders through rocking levers. (Stanier chose his system to avoid distortion of inside valve events from expansion of the outside valve spindle that occurred with rocking levers positioned ahead of the outside cylinders.) Collett had improved upon Churchward's basic shelter for his locomotive crews with a side window cab and Stanier went one better with a double side window cab, although its length was restricted. Stanier designed his own narrow-tube superheater, following Churchward's GWR example, but this did not work well

under LMS operating conditions and was later modified. Bearing in mind the work required from the locomotives, the most significant development was an increase in firebox grate area from 34.3sq ft to 45sq ft; the wider grate made possible only by adoption of the 4-6-2 wheel arrangement. (On 4-6-0s such as the *King* Class the firebox, grate and ashpan have to fit between the frames.) Further dimensions comparing the GWR *King* and LMS *Princess Royal* and *Coronation/Duchess* Classes are included in Appendix One.

Stanier 'imported' a number of Swindon-designed details, inviting inevitable reactionary remarks regarding 'Wiltshire wisdom', but he was never dogmatic and, whenever innovations failed to demonstrate any advantages, they were discontinued. One successful introduction was the side-bearer bogie adopted from the French de Glehn compound 4-cylinder 4-4-2s (although Stanier used bar instead of plate frames to reduce weight) but it was his axlebox design that had the most dramatic impact on the reliability and running costs of LMS locomotives. Prior to his appointment the LMS continued fitting Midland Railway-designed axleboxes (in order to standardise spare parts) which were inadequate for use on heavier or faster trains. After the Stanier axlebox was introduced the number of failures due to 'hot boxes' was reduced by around 90% and the mileage achieved between works visits for major repairs was extended significantly. He incorporated the Midland-pattern injector but, as events proved subsequently, this misplaced loyalty to his new employers was not in the railway's best interests. The 'Midland' injector was less reliable than the GWR-pattern and would become a constant source of trouble. Another problem in the making came from adoption of Ross 'pop-type' safety valves which vented high-pressure steam to the extent of rapidly reducing boiler pressure, often by much more than required for safety but more than enough to compromise superheater efficiency, especially where the degree of superheating was marginal; they may have been one contributory factor in the poor initial performance of his *Jubilee* Class 4-6-0s. (The GWR persevered with its own modification of Ramsbottom's safety valve which, in the hands of skilled crews, could 'sizzle' at maximum boiler pressure without unnecessary and wasteful 'blowing off'.) Domeless boilers were a further Swindon feature (the early dome-like structures housed top-feed clack boxes) with steam collected by perforated tubes in the highest point of the Belpaire firebox 'corners' and delivered to a regulator in the smokebox. The first two 4-6-2s had GWR-type slidebars with forked ends, but these were troublesome and later modified while Nos. 6203-12 had straight ended slidebars from new. As was common GWR practice at the time, all Stanier's early LMS locomotives had vacuum pumps driven from the left-hand outside cylinder crosshead but these were later removed. The LMS and, indeed, all British railways other than the GWR, operated its brakes with a vacuum of '21 inches of mercury' and, for this, continuous operation of the locomotive's small brake ejector effectively dealt with all the inevitable small leaks that occurred. The GWR used '25 inches of mercury' for increased braking pressure and continued using vacuum pumps for many years. One of their disadvantages, compared with ejectors, was that they worked whenever the engine was moving, representing a significant energy loss.

The LMS authorized three of Stanier's new 4-6-2 locomotives and two were completed under Lot No 99 in July/November 1933 as Nos. 6200-1 (later *The Princess Royal* and *Princess Elizabeth*) at a cost of £13,815 each but the frames of No. 6202 were laid aside until it could be completed incorporating steam turbine equipment designed and built by Metropolitan-Vickers. This work was completed in June 1935 under Lot No 100 and at a cost of £20,383; known unofficially as the *Turbomotive* No. 6202 performed well but suffered from being a one-off. Repairs became lengthy as few essential parts were held in stock and in 1952 it was rebuilt as a conventional reciprocating locomotive and named *Princess Anne*. It was damaged beyond economic repair in the disaster at Harrow & Wealdstone in October 1952 but was not condemned until May 1954.

The otherwise impressive appearance of Nos. 6200/1 was ruined by their pairing with modified short MR-pattern straight-sided tenders (with increased coal capacity) but there was logic behind this decision. While longer 8-wheeled tenders would have been more acceptable aesthetically, the resulting combination would have been too long for existing 70-ft turntables, which would have required either expensive extension or even more expensive replacement. The shorter 6-wheeled tender held sufficient coal for the longest trip and water capacity was adequate as the LMS main line was well equipped with troughs for replenishing water supplies at speed (there were eleven sets between Euston and Glasgow) while some schedules

Looking magnificent in LMS livery, No. 6201 Princess Elizabeth *is one of two Stanier 'Princesses' saved for preservation. No. 6201 was rescued for eventual restoration to main line working condition by the* Princess Elizabeth Locomotive Society. *The locomotive's epic runs between London and Glasgow in November 1936 are detailed in Appendix 3 and, on 3 June 2006, almost seventy years later, it was photographed at Carlisle* (Graham Dudley)

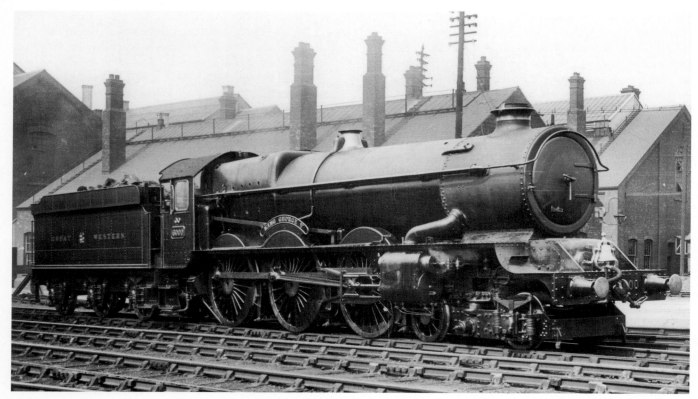

GWR No. 6000 King George V, *with the bell received during its visit to the Baltimore & Ohio Railroad in 1927. Stanier adopted many dimensions from the GWR* King *Class 4-6-0s for his LMS* Princess Royal (Princess Elizabeth) *Class 4-6-2s* (Gresley Society)

allowed northbound trains to stop at Symington, north of Beattock, to take on water. Only three of these tenders were constructed for Nos. 6200-2 although that intended for No. 6202 was fitted to 4-6-0 No. 6100 *Royal Scot* prior to its visit to the USA in 1933 for display at Chicago's 'Century of Progress' Exhibition.

The *Princess Royal* Class was designed at Derby under the direction of Herbert Chambers, then Chief Draughtsman, whose other successes included coordinating

the difficult task of bringing the North British Locomotive Company-built *Royal Scots* into service within the timescale demanded by the LMS Traffic Department, although the detail design of the Pacifics' boiler was credited to J L Francis at Crewe. Chambers was critical of Stanier's selection of GWR-pattern low-degree superheat using only 16 elements and was proved correct – a 32-element superheater was soon substituted which almost doubled the superheater surface area – but his relationship with Stanier

BR No. 46201 Princess Elizabeth, *the second of the two* Princess Royal *prototypes, was photographed while awaiting works attention. It was then painted in an earlier livery with the original BR crest* (Gresley Society)

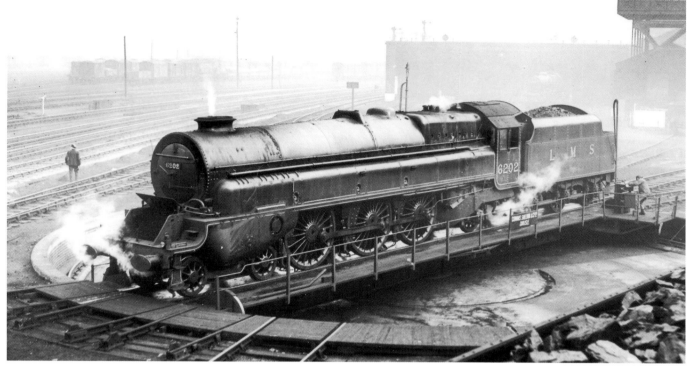

Princess Royal Class No. 6202 was built as a steam turbine experiment and was referred to, unofficially, as 'The Turbomotive'. Ii is seen here at Camden after rebuilding with its second boiler, with separate dome and top feed. The long left-hand casing housed the forward turbine while a smaller reverse turbine was housed on the other side. After rebuilding into BR No. 46202 Princess Anne *in August 1952 it was withdrawn three months later, having been damaged beyond economic repair in the Harrow & Wealdstone disaster*

(Gresley Society)

was soured by this and other disagreements. Chambers was transferred to become Technical Assistant at Euston and was replaced as Chief Draughtsman by T F (Tom) Coleman who had been based at Horwich but now became responsible for drawing offices at both Derby and Crewe.

The GWR's continued adherence to low degree superheat followed lengthy experiments, after which Churchward concluded that superheating beyond the temperature required to prevent condensation in the steam passages was wasteful; lower temperatures meant that regulator sliding surfaces could be lubricated with oil fed into steam before it reached the regulator. This was not possible with high degree superheating as, before development of temperature-resistant lubricants, oil would become 'cooked' or carbonized within superheater elements. After the LMS had adopted high degree superheating, lubrication arrangements were modified so that oil was admitted later in the 'steam cycle', resulting in 'dry' smokebox regulators that were less sensitive than the GWR pattern.

Initially Stanier seemed reluctant to abandon low degree superheat and looked to other means of improving performance. No. 6201 was fitted experimentally with an unusual double chimney with exhaust from inside cylinders directed into one half and that from the outside cylinders passing through the other half, instead of being combined in the blastpipe. This was not a success and usual exhaust arrangements were soon restored, together with a single chimney. The extreme length of the boiler was considered prejudicial to efficient steaming and the distance between tubeplates was decreased from 20ft 9in to 19ft 3in by moving the firebox tubeplate forward, thus extending the firebox into a short combustion chamber and increasing its heating surface area from 190sq ft to 217sq ft. Eventually,

as mentioned above, superheater deficiencies were recognized and, with an increase from 16 to 32 elements, superheater area was increased from 370sq ft to 623sq ft (it would have been more if the tubeplates had remained their original distance apart). According to the minutes of the LMS Locomotive & Electrical Committee, initial low-degree superheating was 'in order to obtain reduced maintenance costs' but that 'work experience had shown (that) a higher degree of superheating will result in an increased operating economy which will more than meet the additional maintenance cost…'.

The 1935 locomotive construction programme was approved in June 1934 and included a further ten 7P 4-6-2s (Nos. 6203-12), all to be built at Crewe under Lot No. 120 at a total cost of £107,000, and these were duly completed between July and November 1935. These new locomotives incorporated modifications developed from experience with the two prototypes but, strangely, while including other boiler improvements, they remained domeless until fitted with new boilers in the 1950s. Nos. 6200/1 were modified with domed boilers around 1935 and the regulator was then transferred to the dome. The original smokebox regulators had a tendency to stick and this was one cause of occasional severe slipping.

Slipping remained a potential problem with all Stanier 4-6-2s even in the most expert hands and, while the observer saw most instances while locomotives were starting heavy trains especially on wet and greasy track, slipping could start at any time and occasionally brought moving trains to a standstill. Smooth metal wheels can progress along smooth metal rails only if the rotational force applied to them remains below the frictional resistance between the two surfaces and, to ensure this, maximum starting tractive effort should not exceed around

Before introduction of electronic data collection systems detailed analysis of locomotive performance depended upon manual recording of parameters such as steam chest and cylinder pressures. Such data was obtained only by the dedicated work of technicians riding in temporary 'indicator shelters' perched at the very front of the locomotives being tested. No. 6209 Princess Beatrice, *from the 'production' series, is seen fitted with shelters early in its LMS career*

(Gresley Society)

25% of the locomotive's adhesion weight (the weight carried by its coupled wheels). This proportion results in a 'factor of adhesion' of four. However, the factor for the GWR *King* Class 4-6-0s was 3.75 and this was adopted by Stanier for both the *Princess Royal* and *Coronation/Duchess* 4-6-2s. While the *Kings* were usually surefooted, Stanier's 4-6-2s certainly were anything but, and the more sensitive GWR regulator was seen as an important factor but there was a more fundamental difference between the two types.

The instant that any turning moment is applied to a locomotive's coupled wheels an equal contra-rotatory moment, applied through the frames, transfers weight to the hindmost axle which, in the case of a 4-6-0, is coupled and therefore has no effect upon overall adhesion weight. Where there is a trailing carrying axle, as on 4-6-2s, the hindmost axle is not coupled and any additional weight transferred to it reduces the weight carried by the coupled wheels, thereby reducing the factor of adhesion. This tendency to slip on

LMS No. 6203 Princess Margaret Rose *photographed at Crewe. This was the first of ten 'production' locomotives built in 1935 after the two prototypes had been in service for two years*

(Gresley Society)

A famous view – Dent on the S&C line with the Duchess *passing through one day in June 1984 with the 'Cumbrian Mountain Express'. The white square on the overbridge was to improve sighting of a signal long removed* (Roger Bastin)

starting has been referred to as 'sitting up and begging' and could be induced by gradients, sharp curvatures, slippery rails (caused by grease, rain, snow or frost) and insensitive regulator use, although the relative ease (or otherwise) with which these worked remained a significant factor.

The *Princess Royals* inherited another problem from their GWR ancestry. Churchward adopted North American practice for his 2-cylinder designs and incorporated interchangeable castings each with a cylinder, valve chest and half of the smokebox saddle; two of these, bolted together, resulted in a solid front end with no possibility of cylinders working loose. This arrangement could not be used with his first 4-cylinder *Star* Class 4-6-0s which had divided drive; the inside cylinders, driving the leading coupled axle, were well ahead of the smokebox while the outer cylinders, driving the centre coupled wheels, were above the trailing wheels of the bogie with all four connecting rods of the same length. Collett continued this arrangement on his *Castle* and *King* Classes as did Stanier with the first LMS 4-6-2s but met with less success, as the outside *Princess* cylinders became loose, even after modifications were made. As will be described later, this problem was resolved with the *Coronations*.

These were all problems inherent in converting the LMS from a 'small engine line' and building its first modern powerful locomotives. (The *Royal Scots* were powerful but, until extensively rebuilt from 1943 onwards, aspects of their design were far from modern.) In service the *Princesses* did all that was expected and were superior to any express locomotive that had previously run over LMS

lines but, inevitably, their success meant that even better performance was required. After the last railway Race to the North (from London to Aberdeen) between the competing East and West Coast routes ended with a derailment at Preston in July 1896, both parties agreed to common schedule of 8¼ hours for the journey between London and Glasgow or Edinburgh but subsequent motive power developments meant that trains were deliberately slowed down in order to comply. With railways facing increasing competition, this farcical situation could not be allowed to continue. After considering German *Fliegende Hamburger* twin-unit diesels for a proposed high-speed service between Leeds or Newcastle and London, Nigel Gresley designed an improved, streamlined version of his A3 4-6-2s and this new A4 Class was introduced in 1935 for the lightweight *Silver Jubilee* service to Newcastle with a train of articulated streamlined carriages but this was only the beginning. More A4s were being built together with another streamlined train (this time with nine instead of seven carriages) for the LNER's 6-hour *Coronation* service between London and Edinburgh starting in 1937.

The LMS had to respond and, in November 1936, No. 6201 *Princess Elizabeth* was prepared for two high-speed non-stop test runs to establish whether the 401½-mile trip between Euston and Glasgow was possible within a 6-hour schedule. The train was in the hands of Driver T J Clarke and Fireman C Fleet, both of Crewe, together with an inspector (who assisted with the firing) and Robin Riddles, who had prepared a continuous roller map for monitoring progress. Riddles worked through

29

In 1937 Princess Royal Class *No. 6205* Princess Victoria *was rebuilt with both sets of inside Walschaert motion replaced by rocking levers operated from the outside valve gear. The modified motion bracket can be seen on this photograph of the locomotive in early BR livery*   *(Gresley Society)*

Princess Royal Class *No. 6208* Princess Helena Victoria *(a little confusing as No. 6205 was named* Princess Victoria*) was in immaculate ex-works condition when photographed at Crewe*   *(Gresley Society)*

much of the night of the 15/16 November after a main steam pipe joint failed while No. 6201 was being prepared at Willesden and this was repaired with a replacement stainless steel coned joint sent late that night from Crewe. Once the train arrived at Glasgow routine examination revealed that the GWR-type forked slidebars had again caused overheating problems and the white metal lining in left-hand slide block had melted and run out, giving Riddles another sleepless night, this time at St Rollox Works.

In terms of time, the trial was a total success and full details of distances and timing points for these quite amazing trips (down and up) are included as Appendix 3. In reality it was recognized that the special preparation and effort that went into the trial were not sustainable in normal daily running, especially as the need for a number of track improvements had been identified. The fast service between Euston and Glasgow would be delayed until 1937 when new and improved locomotives would be available – and, for publicity reasons at least, these would have to be streamlined.

30

A more familiar form of streamlining. LNER No. 4468 Mallard *at Doncaster when newly completed in March 1938*   (*NRM Collection*)

Streamlining railway locomotives was not a new idea. Dr Dionysius Lardner FRS carried out tests on the Grand Junction Railway but, in a paper presented to the British Association for the Advancement of Science in 1841, he concluded that 'expedients for attaching a sharp front to the engine are ineffectual and useless', a statement that was undoubtedly true at the time. As train speeds increased there was an increased awareness of the energy required to overcome wind resistance but the earliest practical application of streamlining did not appear until 1888. T. Ricour, chief mechanical engineer on the French Etat Railway, found that an air-smoothed casing reduced wind resistance by about 10% at speeds in excess of 60mph. while Adolphe Henry's final design for the Paris, Lyons and Mediterranean Railway, a four-cylinder compound 4-4-0, appeared in 1892 with streamlined features that included a wedge-shaped front to both smokebox and chimney. These, the celebrated *Coupevents*, were designed to overcome the formidable *Mistral* as it blew up the Rhône Valley.

There were few subsequent developments until the dawning of the 'Streamline Age' in the late 1920s when streamlining became a 'must' for anything representing new technology. Private motor car ownership was increasing and manufacturers vied with each other to provide more attractive shapes although here, as elsewhere, efficient function was often sacrificed to form. The civil airline industry was attracting passengers with futuristic streamlined aircraft and even domestic appliances were expected to conform to this latest image of modernity. Railways, faced with the real pressure of improved road transport and potential competition from air travel, looked to streamlining as much to modernize their image rather than to provide faster services. As an aside it is curious to note that some early developments occurred under totalitarian regimes without unregulated competition.

The twin pressures of competition and consumerism were, perhaps, greatest in the United States where streamlined Brill electric railcars were introduced in

An official works photograph of the second of the class – No. 6221 Queen Elizabeth *–immediately after completion in June 1937. The was one of the five 'blue streamliners' and operated from Glasgow for much of its working life*
          (*Gresley Society*)

Duchess of Hamilton crosses the Ribble at Helwith Bridge (between Stainforth and Horton in Ribblesdale) during June 1984   (Roger Bastin)

1931 for the 14-mile route between Philadelphia and Norristown, their design having first been tested in Michigan University's wind tunnel. In 1932 Germany introduced a streamlined diesel railcar with twin Maybach 410bhp engines which, when operating the *Fliegende Hamburger* service, covered the 178 miles between Berlin and Hamburg at an average speed of around 77mph. France was not to be outdone as Ettore Bugatti, needing an extra outlet for the 12.766 litre 200bhp petrol engines built for his glorious but commercially unsuccessful Type 41 *Royale* motor cars (only six were built), installed four in each streamlined *Presidentiel* railcar, one of which achieved a world rail speed record of 196km per hour on the Paris-Strasbourg line in 1937. The last of the 79 Bugatti railcars was not withdrawn until 1958.

While electric, diesel and petrol propulsion achieved these initial successes, steam was not excluded. Under the expansionist Japanese regime of the early 1900s mainland Manchuria (renamed Manchukuo by the Japanese) was occupied and many railways were converted to standard gauge (from the broader Russian gauge). The *Asia Express* service over the 438-mile line between Dairen (now Dalian) and Hsingking (now Changchun) began in 1934 using streamlined steam 4-6-2s and air-conditioned coaches built to an advanced specification. In Britain, meanwhile, the LNER considered buying German-built diesel railcars introduced between Berlin and Hamburg but the builders, Wagen und Maschinenbau AG, believed the LNER's combination of gradients and speed restrictions would limit average speeds to 63mph, resulting in a 165-minute schedule between Leeds and London (King's Cross), but with much depending upon the culinary expectations of the travelling public. German businessmen were satisfied with a cold buffet trolley service but their British counterparts expected more traditional (and substantial) hot fare served in a restaurant car; this would have been impossible using the proposed *Fliegende Hamburger* diesel railcars. As an alternative Sir Nigel

Gresley experimented with a short lightweight formation (including a restaurant and kitchen car) hauled by a steam locomotive and, on 30 November 1934, A1 Class 4-6-2 No. 4472 *Flying Scotsman* covered the 185.8 miles from King's Cross to Leeds (similar to the distance between Berlin and Hamburg) with a special four-coach train in just under 152 minutes, a record that stood for over thirty years. The return run, made on the same day but with a six-coach train, saw 100mph officially recorded for the first time with steam (*City of Truro's* 1904 record was not supported by dynamometer car evidence) with a start-to-finish time of just over 157 minutes. On 5 March 1935 a further trial with No. 2750 *Papyrus* demonstrated that six-coach trains could be run between King's Cross and Newcastle (268.3 miles) within a four-hour schedule. On the return journey an authenticated 108mph maximum was recorded at Essendine.

These trials resulted in the development of Gresley's A4 Class 4-6-2s, introduced in 1935 initially for working four-hour trains between King's Cross and Newcastle, the schedule allowing for an intermediate stop at Darlington. The locomotives were developed from the A1/A3 Class with an increased boiler pressure of 250psi but their most noticeable feature was a streamlined casing incorporating the wedge-shaped front introduced by Ettore Bugatti. For this new high-speed *Silver Jubilee* service (named to commemorate the 25th year of the reign of King George V) Gresley built light-weight articulated coaches with fairings between bogies (with flexible fairings between coaches) to reduce aerodynamic drag. For PR purposes the 'Silver' theme was developed with the first four locomotives having 'silver' names (*Silver Link*, *Quicksilver*, *Silver King* and *Silver Fox*) and all received a silver-grey livery while the carriages were covered in matching 'American cloth' or 'Rexine'. The LNER scored a major public relations success not only through its high-speed services but with its adoption of streamlining and application of a modernistic livery to both locomotive and train. The LMS, concerned first to protect and then develop its Anglo-Scottish business, had to respond and had to repeat much of the LNER's basic research.

Gresley's streamlined design represented more than just a novel eye-catching shape; it was the outcome of serious scientific study. Scale models of non-streamlined A3s and various streamlined options were compared within the National Physical Laboratory's wind tunnel before the new design was finalized and the results indicated that streamlining could improve both performance and economy. Streamlining reduced the power required to overcome head-on air resistance by 41hp at 60mph to 639hp at 150mph, this latter test simulating a locomotive running at maximum speed directly into a very strong headwind. Assuming continuous high-speed running at 80-90mph, these results equated to fuel savings of around 4lb (1.8Kg) per mile, equivalent to 200 tons per year, more than enough to offset all increased maintenance costs created by the streamlined casing.

Smooth air conditions, or laminar flow, used for these tests are never replicated outside of wind tunnels or similar artificial devices and it is unlikely that anything approaching these theoretical savings were ever made. Handrails, lamps, buffers, couplings and cab openings were essential appendages that detracted from aerodynamic efficiency by inducing localized vortices while the aerodynamic drag from the train increased exponentially with speed. Furthermore, Britain's prevailing westerly winds meant that true head-on air resistance was rarely encountered on north-south routes while turbulence from trackside features and buildings was a further complication; under extreme conditions air-smoothed casings could actually increase rolling resistance, especially with side winds. However, even if results in practice were never as good as predicted, Gresley's streamlining produced one vital benefit; under most conditions it lifted exhaust smoke and steam clear of the cab, giving drivers an unrestricted view of the road ahead.

Stanier regarded external streamlining with some ambivalence. Under Churchward the GWR developed a 'no-nonsense' approach to locomotive design and its commitment to efficient function left little scope for cosmetic detailing. In 1935 C B Collett, Churchward's successor, received a request from the GWR Locomotive Committee (but probably originating with the railway's powerful publicity department) for streamlined locomotives and his response was almost contemptuous. According to legend he smeared plasticine around a paperweight model of a *King* 4-6-0, smoothing and fairing projecting external features and adding a hemispherical smokebox front; this was then sent for drawings to be made. The resulting appearance was ludicrous. Nos. 6014 *King Henry VII* and 5005 *Manorbier Castle* appeared in this strange guise, but only for a few months as many additional features were incompatible with proper maintenance. Collett's reaction might have been extreme but it typified the GWR's approach to unnecessary design 'frills' and, of course, Stanier was deeply immersed in Swindon philosophy. Nevertheless he was convinced that, like it or not (and, reputedly, he loathed it!), he and the LMS had to follow Gresley's initiative towards scientific streamlining.

The LMS Board appeared to share Stanier's initial lack of enthusiasm as, on 30 July 1936, it approved construction of 'an additional five *Princess*-type

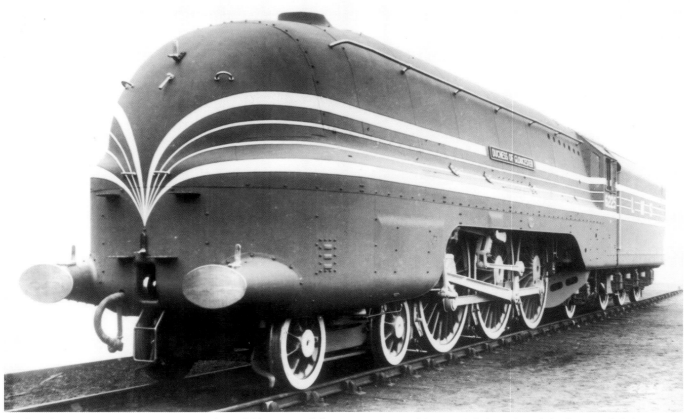

The first of the 'red streamliners' – No. 6225 Duchess of Gloucester *– before entering service in May 1938. The louvred panel (for the proposed ATC apparatus) can be seen behind the left buffer. Note the leading step and the recessed coupling; coupling the locomotive from the front was difficult and extremely hazardous as clearance was negligible*

(Gresley Society)

Inside Crewe Works during early 1938. On the left is the almost completed No. 6228 Duchess of Rutland *which entered service in June 1938. To the right is the partially streamlined* Duchess of Hamilton. *Photographs such as these provided the re-streamlining team at Tyseley with valuable information, especially over matters such as the shape and construction of crinoline irons, i.e. the 'hoops' holding the streamlined casing away from the boiler* (Gresley Society)

locomotives' as part of the 1937 building programme. Stanier decided that these should be of an improved design (and, bowing to what he considered to be inevitable, accepted that these should be streamlined) as trials with No. 6201 *Princess Elizabeth* had demonstrated that while non-stop 6-hour services between London (Euston) and Glasgow were feasible, they could only be operated by existing locomotives if specially prepared. More powerful locomotives were required if the proposed high-speed service was to begin in 1937 but, with Stanier serving on a Government Commission in India, much of the necessary design work was delegated to Coleman and his staff, with Riddles acting as Stanier's representative. The official account acknowledged that the class was designed by 'the drawing office staffs at Crewe and Derby' instead of giving the traditional credit to the CME. It was Coleman who designed the streamlined casing for what would become the *Coronation* Class but it was only after the manufacturing drawings had been issued to Crewe Works that Sir Harold Hartley was informed, and he insisted upon full wind tunnel testing to ensure selection of the most efficient shape. Drawings for different scale models were prepared for testing in the wind tunnel at the LMS Scientific Research Laboratory at Derby under direction of F C Johansen, formerly of the NPL, but it appears that the only model actually made was to Coleman's original design; fortunately test performances were good and better than Gresley's A4s in one respect. The bulbous front disturbed the air less than Gresley's wedge-fronted design but this meant less clearance of exhaust gases and, as confirmed by photographs, smoke often drifted into the driver's line of vision. Overall, however, improvements in aerodynamic

efficiency were estimated as equivalent to fuel savings of £300 each year per locomotive but, with the Board continuing to vacillate, Coleman resubmitted drawings without streamlined casings but with a *Lady Godiva* nameplate! The point was made and approval was granted for streamlining but, while this particular battle was won, the war was far from over and would ultimately be lost.

The first five locomotives of the *Princess Coronation* class (the official LMS title) were completed in 1937 (building dates for the whole class are given in Appendix 2) and were finished in a striking blue livery with silver horizontal stripes. The colour is often described as 'Caley Blue', a shade difficult to define with precision. The original Caledonian Railway livery was deep ultramarine blue, using expensive pigments, but became lighter over the years (according to one account increasing amounts of 'free issue' white paint were added unofficially as a paint shop economy measure) but the colour confirmed the locomotives' intended role on the principal Anglo-Scottish expresses. The lining (two broad horizontal silver bands enclosing two narrower bands) started as a merged 'V' just above the leading coupling then swept along the locomotive and tender and continued along the train. Unlike the rival LNER, the LMS began its prestige London to Scotland expresses without specially built carriages but depended on existing designs, converted with luxurious internal facilities, pressure ventilation and, of course, special livery. A train of purpose-built articulated carriages was completed in 1939 for use on the *Coronation Scot* but, after display at the New York World Fair, it was marooned in America until after the war. The five 'blue' locomotives were based at Camden when new but from

34

1939 all were transferred to Glasgow (Polmadie) where they remained for many years. Tenders were also streamlined with side plates extended rearwards in line with rear buffer faces and with sliding doors at the top rear of each side providing access to water tank fillers. The front part of the coal space was covered with a cowl with the same profile as the cab roof to reduce footplate draughts while additional air-smoothing was provided by a skirting beneath the tender tank covering the springs while leaving axleboxes exposed.

Ten more 'Coronation-type' locomotives were authorized for construction during 1938, the first five of which, including No. 6229 *Duchess of Hamilton*, were streamlined. On these the livery was even more handsome, consisting of crimson lake (based upon Midland Railway passenger livery) with gold stripes applied as described above. Nos. 6230-34, forming the second group, were never streamlined as they were designed for the heaviest passenger trains, instead of the faster, lighter and more prestigious services. Lord Stamp did not approve and considered that the publicity value of streamlining was worth more to the LMS than the £300 costs incurred from fabricating the three-ton streamlined casing and, as a consequence, the next fourteen were streamlined. After Lord Stamp's death followed, in 1942, by Stanier's secondment as Scientific Adviser to the wartime Ministry of Production, streamlining lost support on the LMS. The railway's running sheds had always been less than enthusiastic as streamlined casings restricted access to parts needing daily attention and routine maintenance took longer. The final nine locomotives were built without streamlined casings although the first four were coupled to already-constructed streamlined tenders.

During the war years it was impossible to maintain attractive liveries and many streamlined locomotives appeared later in an unattractive overall matt black unrelieved by lining. In their frequent grimy and unkempt condition they added nothing to the railway's prestige and, with wartime and early postwar trains limited to 75mph (at which speed streamlining would be of little benefit), de-streamlining was the only option, especially as this would improve maintenance access. Nothing was done, however, until 1945, when No. 6235 had its streamlined casing removed but afterwards progress was rapid and few passed to British Railways in streamlined form. No. 46229 *Duchess of Hamilton* was in Crewe Works at the time of the handover and emerged devoid of its casing while No. 46243 *City of Lancaster* was the last streamliner to remain in service as such. Its casing was removed during a works visit in 1949. De-streamlining was a relatively easy procedure as, unlike Gresley's A4 4-6-2s, there was a conventional locomotive underneath the casing as confirmed by the works photograph on page 34.

At first the de-streamlined engines did not assume the majesty of the original non-streamlined members of the class as they had one unusual and unattractive feature. To fit within the streamlined casing, the smokebox top was 'bevelled' and de-streamlined locomotives retained their odd sloping smokeboxes until replacements of more conventional pattern were required. In this 'half-and-half' phase they were sometimes referred to (entirely unofficially) as 'semis' (i.e. semi-streamlined). At one stage during re-streamlining work *Duchess of Hamilton*, with its smokebox newly cut down to the required profile, was positioned outside Tyseley Works to provide a unique photo-opportunity of a 'semi'.

Posing as a 'semi', Duchess of Hamilton *was positioned outside Tyseley Works on May 6th, 2006. This side of the locomotive was painted in LMS postwar black livery specifically for the visit by the 229 Club*

(*Ian R. Smith*)

Duchess of Hamilton *changed identities with LMS No. 6220* Coronation *prior to its North American visit. Here the 'genuine'* Coronation, *as confirmed by the absence of louvred ventilation panels, is seen at Crewe North in travel-stained blue livery*
(Gresley Society)

The West Coast main line had severe gradients with few stretches of track suitable for sustained high speed running so that, to meet the proposed ambitious 6-hour schedule, the new locomotive needed good hill climbing ability as there was little opportunity to regain lost time by running fast downhill. This was possible only by using a boiler even larger than on the *Princess* class and, using its increased capacity as a reservoir while climbing gradients, steam could be used faster than it could be generated – but only as long as water within the boiler, and surrounding the firebox, remained at a safe level. (Using steam faster than its production rate is referred to as 'mortgaging the boiler'.) Two problems had to be overcome before a larger boiler could be fitted; firstly it had to comply with the existing loading gauge and, secondly, overall weight had to be within the 22$^{1}/_{2}$ tons axle load imposed by the LMS civil engineer, a limit already reached with the *Princesses*.

A nominal coupled wheel diameter of 6ft 9in was selected (actual wheel diameter varied depending upon the tyres – it could increase by 4-6in when new tyres were fitted) and the boiler's outside diameter was increased to a maximum of 6ft 5$^{1}/_{2}$in compared with 6ft 3in on the *Princess* Class. These changes increased the boiler's centre line to 9ft 6in above rail level but it remained possible to accommodate everything within the loading gauge – but only just. (With the streamlined casing in place, the maximum height above rail level was 13ft 2$^{5}/_{8}$in with just a fraction of an inch to spare.) The boiler, designated 1X by the LMS (the *Princesses* had Class 1 boilers), was built with

two tapered rings as before but the main difference was in using nickel steel alloy for its construction. This alloy included nickel (1.75 to 2.0%) and manganese (0.5 to 0.7%) and, while similarly sized ingots weighed the same as carbon steel, its use produced a weight reduction of two tons because of its increased strength. (As 2% nickel steel withstands a maximum stress of 34-38 tons/sq in compared with 26-30 tons for carbon steel, thinner boiler plates compromised neither strength nor safety.) Other weight savings were achieved by using 'Vibrac' steel for coupling and connecting rods. Copper was used for inner firebox construction and this was held apart from the outer firebox casing mainly by steel stays although outer top rows and the throat plate had Monel Metal stays. As before, the distance between tubeplates was 19ft 3in and, once again, the firebox was extended into the boiler barrel to form a combustion chamber. The regulator was dome-mounted but, with reduced clearance, it was necessary to fit baffle plates beneath the dome to prevent entrained water entering the steam pipe. There were two injectors, both with 13mm cones; the exhaust steam injector, running on steam that had already been used in the cylinders, was used throughout each journey for 'topping up' and was on the fireman's side while the live steam injector, used for replenishing larger volumes, was on the driver's side. (Whenever possible, the live steam injector was used only while the locomotive was stationary as its use while running detracted from its available power.) Both supplied the boiler through top feed clack boxes, the water being first

A photograph of No. 6222 Queen Mary *taken soon after completion in June 1937 with its blue livery (with silver stripes) unblemished. It was the least used of all members of the class; by the time of its withdrawal in October 1963 it had achieved an average annual mileage of 55,723, an impressive figure but still well below the class average*

(Gresley Society)

delivered on to trays within the steam space to boil off dissolved gases. Four 2¹/₂-inch diameter Ross pop safety valves were mounted above the firebox.

All major dimensions are tabulated in Appendix One but some increases deserve special mention. Compared with the *Princess* class, the heating surface area of the small tubes was increased from 1,272 to 1,545sq ft, that of the large tubes or flues from 825 to 1,032sq ft and the firebox heating surface area, including combustion chamber, was 230 instead of 217sq ft resulting in a massive evaporative heating surface of 2,807sq ft. Each of the 40 flues contained three 1-in outside diameter elements with a combined surface area of 856sq ft (later reduced to 830sq ft) compared with the 653sq ft of the *Princess* class, even after

modification, while grate area was also increased from 45 to 50sq ft. Boiler pressure remained the same at 250psi.

In all forty-four class 1X boilers were eventually built for the thirty-eight *Coronation/Duchess* class locomotives; boilers were usually exchanged during heavy general repairs and, with boiler repairs (and subsequent testing) requiring most workshop time, fitting new or previously overhauled spare boilers resulted in an earlier return to traffic. Most but not all new engines entered service with newly-constructed boilers and the earlier members of the class had around nine boiler changes during their life. Boiler numbers were 9937-41(built 1937), 10287-306 (1938), 10637-46 (built between around 1940 to 1944), 10693-4 (1944), 12470-4 (1946-48) and 13043-4

LMS No. 6222 Queen Mary *at Crewe North after de-streamlining. This photograph illustrates the sloping smokebox top carried for a few years by de-streamlined engines, the open front footplating and the austere but elegant LMS postwar express passenger livery*

(Gresley Society)

(1949-50). Although the smokebox top was bevelled to fit the casing profile on streamlined engines there was no difference in the boilers proper, which were fully interchangeable between streamlined and non-streamlined locomotives.

The leading four-wheeled bogie was, once again, Stanier's modified version of the GWR Churchward-de Glehn type with side bolsters transmitting the load from the frames while the trailing two-wheeled truck was of the Bissell-type (first patented in the USA by Levi Bissell in 1858) with its arm pivoted on the cross stretcher immediately in front of the firebox tubeplate. The side bearers for this worked within two sets of separate plates spliced to the main frames and carried through to the rear buffer beam with the inner plates splayed inwards and the outer plates outwards. This arrangement was not entirely satisfactory as plate fractures developed over time. The last two locomotives built under Ivatt had a revised rear-end arrangement incorporating cast steel components. Coupled wheel diameter was increased from the 6ft 6in of the *Princess* class to 6ft 9in as, with the locomotive expected to run faster, it was considered desirable to reduce piston speed. (Cylinder efficiency decreases after a given piston speed; the increased wheel diameter was enough to reduce piston speed by around 3.7% for any given track speed.) Robin Riddles is reputed to have recommended the larger diameter to give the locomotive 'longer legs' at speed but, by his own admission, he had 'forgotten that the engine had to start from a stand; and could those big wheels slip!'. Their axleboxes were steel castings with pressed-in bronze liners lined with white-metal (tin 85%, antimony 10%, copper 5%) on the bearing surface and, as mentioned earlier, these made a significant contribution to the trouble-free running of all Stanier's locomotives.

The larger wheels would have decreased nominal tractive effort from the *Princess Royals'* 40,300lbs to 38,800lbs had all other relevant dimensions remained unaltered so, in order to compensate, cylinder diameter was increased by 0.25 inch to 16^1/$_2$in, resulting in a tractive effort of 40,000lbs. Piston valve diameter was 9in with maximum valve travel of 7^1/$_{32}$in in full gear; valve actuation was by two sets of Walschaert motion situated outside of the frames directly driving the outside piston valves and driving the inside piston valves indirectly through rocking levers. To overcome Stanier's objection to levers worked through extended valve spindles, Coleman devised an arrangement by which rocking levers were connected to outside valve spindles ahead of the combination lever pivot, where there would be less risk of inside valve events being distorted by expansion. All valve motion parts had Hoffman needle bearings other than the eccentric rod big ends, which had Skefko self-aligning ball bearings.

On the *Princess* class both inside and outside connecting rods were of similar length to ensure an equal balance of reciprocating masses but the disadvantage was that the outside cylinders were positioned over the rear bogie wheels from where the cylinders worked loose over time. Coleman altered the arrangement on the *Coronation* class; outside cylinders were moved forward so that their front casting could be bolted to the rear of the inside cylinder casting, resulting in a more solid and secure construction. The apparent disadvantage of dissimilar connecting rod lengths was less important with four-cylinder locomotives; in any case compensation for out-of-balance forces on individual axles could be applied during balancing. As it was, 50% of the reciprocating weights were balanced, equally divided between the coupled wheels, together with full balancing of rotating parts such as cranks, crank pins and coupling rods. Balancing was achieved by rotating wheel-sets at speed within a balancing rig and adding increasing amounts of molten lead to pockets formed between plates bolted to both sides of several adjacent spokes. The plates provided the basic balance calculated using nominal values with lead added as required for fine adjustments; this method had largely replaced using integrally cast balance weights.

Duchess *and train dwarfed by the mighty Ribblehead Viaduct – June 1984*

(Roger Bastin)

No. 46251 City of Nottingham *visited Swindon on 9 May 1964 with the RCTS Special. Despite its gleaming condition, it was withdrawn for scrapping just four months later*
(T J Edgington Collection)

The locomotives' ability to run smoothly at speed without causing track damage through high 'hammer blows' confirmed that balancing was effective.

The *Coronation* class benefited from two forms of streamlining. External streamlining, dealt with elsewhere, was immediately apparent and of importance from the publicity point of view but had little effect upon performance other than at high speeds. Internal streamlining of steam passages was of benefit irrespective of track speed and Gresley, Stanier and Riddles all followed the example of André Chapelon, once described as 'The Genius of French Steam'. Chapelon established that efficiency could be improved by increasing the cross-sectional area of steam circuits from regulator to exhaust, reducing the distance travelled by steam, by improving steam pipe shapes so that unavoidable bends had the largest possible radius and by proper calculation of the volume of all intermediate pipes. For example, if the volume of pipes supplying steam to piston valves is inadequate then efficiency is decreased by 'throttling' while, if exhaust passages have excessive volume, they become reservoirs, increasing back-pressure and reducing efficiency. One manifestation of such streamlining could be seen on engines built without streamlined casings before smoke

An impressive view of Duchess of Hamilton *at Mallerstang with the 'Cumbrian Mountain Express' during September 1990*
(Roger Bastin)

LMS No. 6230 Duchess of Buccleuch *was the first of the class to be built in non-streamlined form. It is seen soon after completion at Crewe in June 1938 with its original single chimney and, consequently, with no smoke deflector plates* *(Gresley Society)*

No. 6232 Duchess of Montrose *appeared in 'photographic grey' livery immediately after completion at Crewe in July 1938. The impressive appearance of the non-streamlined locomotive was spoiled to some extent by the array of lubricators and sandbox fillers above the platform. Note the curved plating connecting the platforms behind the buffer beam and above the coupled wheels* *(Gresley Society)*

deflectors were fitted; the smokebox could be seen to nestle within a massive casting that connected it to all four cylinders and enclosed bifurcated steam pipes having both large diameter and curvature. The smokebox was carefully designed to keep the bottom free from as many obstructions as possible to facilitate removal of ash and 'char' and also to have a straight blastpipe in line with the original single chimney. This was, perhaps, the only major area where improvement was necessary. In February 1939 No. 6234 *Duchess of Abercorn* was fitted experimentally with a double blastpipe and chimney; the improvement in

performance was such that all existing members of the class were converted and double chimneys appeared from new on all later locomotives. (This was a relatively simple arrangement with twin blastpipes discharging in line with twin chimneys and did not incorporate the complex cowls and spreaders of the Kylchap exhaust ejector used, for example, on Gresley's streamlined A4s.)

Steam braking was provided for the locomotive with brake blocks acting on the front of each coupled wheel and compensated to give equal pressure on each. The driver controlled application of both the engine's steam brake and

No. 6235 City of Birmingham *was the first of the class to be built from new with a double chimney and, during 1945, it was the first to be de-streamlined. It was photographed in immaculate late-LMS unlined black livery prior to re-entering service* (Gresley Society)

the train's vacuum brake through a valve with a proportional (or 'graduable') action that ensured that, for reasons of safety, the locomotive continued to pull its train under braking without being pushed. According to the maker's original brochure, this was 'achieved automatically by applying air pressure to the vacuum pipe to regulate steam pressure in the brake cylinder'. As with the *Princess* class the first five members of the *Coronation* class were fitted with vacuum pumps when new but these were removed from 1938 onwards. It had been found that the combined ejectors (with separate valves controlling steam to the large and small ejectors) functioned satisfactorily without the pumps; it also was thought that the pumps were a contributory factor whenever the left-hand piston rod (used to drive the pump) fractured in the crosshead.

Steam sanding was one of the major developments of the late 19th century (Holt, the Derby works manager, was credited with its introduction on the Midland Railway in 1886) and it was used on the LMS prior to Stanier's appointment. The GWR preferred dry sanding by gravity (it was sometimes referred to as 'mechanical trickle sanding') and this was another Swindon practice introduced by Stanier that proved unsatisfactory in LMS service. Sand available for locomotive use did not always have the necessary free-running qualities but, even when dry, it could be blown away by strong cross winds on exposed locations such as Shap or Beattock. From 1938 the LMS substituted steam sanding gear on locomotives previously dependent upon gravity sanding and, of course, it was fitted on all newly-built designs such as the *Coronation* class, which had sand supplied to the front of the leading and middle coupled wheels to assist forward running and to the rear of the middle wheel for use when reversing. At least

the first five locomotives were fitted with another sand-dispensing device – a sand gun – one of the very few gadgets to be introduced by Stanier. Intended to clean the tubes while running, it consisted of a valve mounted on the firedoor plate with a wide ferrule passing through the inner firebox copper wall. When steam was admitted, sand was picked up from a container and blasted into the firebox through a nozzle, the angle of which could be rotated within the ferrule. According to reports its use brought about 'a good showing of soot' so it seems to have been effective!

The tenders were modified versions of those used on the later *Princesses* with the same coal and water capacity (10 tons and 4,000 gallons respectively) but there was one important difference. Firemen experienced problems with the earlier tenders in bringing coal forward towards the end of a run and so this latest design was fitted with a coal pusher powered by a $10^{1}/_{2}$-inch diameter steam cylinder positioned in the top rear of the coal space. Its operation was controlled by the fireman through a regulator and saved considerable manual effort; it was sufficiently successful to be adopted by Riddles for the larger capacity BR standard tenders. As usual the tender had steam brakes, acting through brake blocks on the rear of each wheel, and these could also be applied manually by the tender handbrake. Water pick-up gear was provided (long-distance runs would have been impossible with such a small tender were it not for the ability to replenish water from troughs at up to eleven points along the route) with the scoop fitted with a deflector to reduce the volume of water wasted through being splashed sideways.

There were three main tender designs used on the *Coronation* class. Twenty-eight (Nos. 9703-7, 9743-7 and

The Duchesses *were not relegated from working main line express trains until their final years. Here, No. 46245* City of London *heads an up parcels train through Rugby around 1962*

(*J T Edgington Collection*)

Close up of Duchess of Sutherland *showing the point, just in front of the combination lever top, where the rocking lever is driven from the outside valve spindle*

(*John S Hobbs*)

Duchess of Sutherland – *The driver's 'office'*

(*John S Hobbs*)

9798-815) were of Type A which were streamlined with all flat plates, stiffening angles and partitions assembled by electrical welding. The extent of streamlining included incorporation of an air-smoothed valance below the tank that fully covered the springs, extension of the sideplates rearwards to be in line with the tender buffer faces, thus reducing the gap (and much resulting drag-inducing turbulence) between tender and train and fitting a cowl over the front top of the bunker (restricting its opening to 11ft 7³/₄in) to reduce footplate draughts. Sliding doors on either side of the rear casing gave access for filling the tank from water cranes. As mentioned elsewhere, four tenders had been built for Nos. 6249-52 before the decision had been taken to discontinue streamlining and these non-streamlined locomotives ran for a while with streamlined tenders. Five tenders numbered 9748-52 were of Type B, similar to Type A, but non-streamlined while the remaining five were classified Type C (Nos. 9816-7 and 10622-4) which were non-streamlined with partly riveted tank construction. Type C was divided into parts 1 and 2 depending upon the shape of the cut-away at the front of the sideplates, the last two having a noticeably lower cut-away.

Arguments supporting streamlining were outlined earlier and, as also mentioned, wartime exigencies were an important factor in removal of the streamlined casings. Even after the bevelled smokeboxes of the de-streamlined locomotives had been replaced there remained minor differences to indicate the original state of any locomotive or tender. On the original five built without streamlining (Nos. 6230-4) platforms above the coupled wheels and behind the leading buffer beam were joined with curved plating but this was omitted on rebuilt engines and those built after 1944. De-streamlined tenders had neither steps behind the rear wheels nor their accompanying vertical handrails but there was a vertical ladder fixed to the back of the tender tank. It was, presumably, difficult to cut back the

extended sidesheets to make them flush with the tender back and, as a consequence, they remained proud by a few inches.

Tests both on the road and, later, in Rugby's static test plant confirmed that the *Coronation* Class, in common with other later British Pacific locomotives, could generate power far in excess of what was required in normal service but that this surplus power could not be utilized for more than short periods because of the limitations of hand-firing with a single fireman. It is sad to reflect that such impressive potential could never be properly realized without mechanical stokers and, in their absence, such unrealized potential had no commercial value. (This reflection is not intended to denigrate a single fireman's skill in carefully preparing his fire preparatory to a big 'push' nor does it ignore the limitations of mechanical stokers.) It was therefore surprising that, during 1938, the Derby drawing office was considering an even more powerful locomotive based upon principles developed in France by André Chapelon. It would have been a 4-cylinder compound with inside high-pressure and outside low-pressure cylinders with oscillating cam poppet valve gear, Kylchap double exhaust and an even larger boiler. (It is interesting to note that, in 1926, the LMS approved construction of five 4-cylinder compound Pacifics; this scheme was cancelled at short notice and, instead, the North British Locomotive Company was awarded a design-and-build contract for what became the *Royal Scot* 4-6-0s.) Later the proposed larger boiler was replaced by a higher pressure (300psi) version of the *Coronation* Type 1X boiler and, later still, all thoughts of compounding were dismissed although the higher pressure was retained, as were the slightly smaller cylinders necessary for producing the same tractive effort, together with incorporation of Houlet superheater elements.

Production of the last two non-streamlined locomotives from the 1939 programme was held back so

No. 46229 Duchess of Hamilton *still retaining its sloping-top smokebox, near Carlisle with the* 'Royal Scot'   (Gordon Turner, Lanchester, Co. Durham)

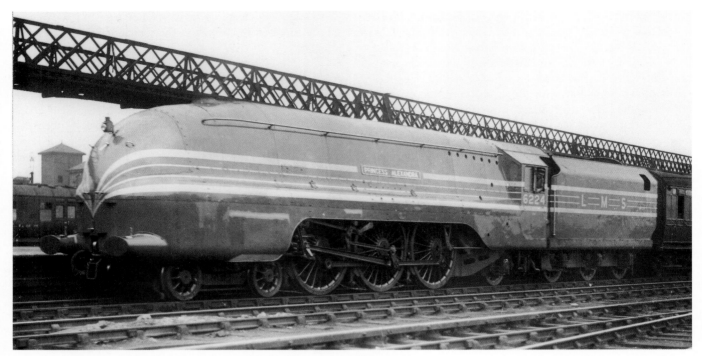

LMS No. 6224 Princess Alexandra *was completed in July 1937 as the last of the five 'blue streamliners', all of which were intended for fast expresses between London and Glasgow. Unusually for the period,* Princess Alexandra *carries the headlamp code for an 'ordinary' (i.e. non-express) passenger train. When photographed at Crewe the sliding door (at the rear of the tender) providing access for filling the tank was either open (unusual) or missing (even more unusual)*

(Gresley Society)

This profile of recently de-streamlined LMS No. 6242 City of Glasgow *well illustrates the double chimney, sloping smokebox, cut-away front framing and postwar livery of the rebuilt locomotives*

(Gresley Society)

that these modifications could be included but the project was cancelled at the outbreak of war and the order was not reinstated until 1946. By this time it was decided that this final pair, Nos. 6256/7, should be used in competition with a 'trial diesel-electric locomotive of 3,200hp in the form of two bogie-mounted units each of 1,600hp coupled together.' (These entered service as LMS Nos. 10000/1.) Nos. 6256/7 were extensively modified by Ivatt to reflect postwar operating conditions and, while including none of the developments proposed initially, they had rocking grates, self-emptying ashpans and self-cleaning fireboxes. Timken tapered roller bearings were fitted throughout other than on the crank axlebox, where the Skefko type was employed. The original design of rear spliced frame-plates supporting the

firebox had suffered from occasional fractures and was replaced with a cast-steel bar frame structure, a new type of reversing gear cut-off indicator was fitted in the cab (this used a revolving drum instead of markings engraved on a flat plate; it continued in use on all BR Standard locomotives) and the superheater was redesigned to provide an unprecedented 979sq ft of heating surface.

The last locomotive to be completed was No. 46257 *City of Salford*, which was completed at Crewe on 19 May 1948 and was therefore always owned by British Railways. The last of the class to be completed by the LMS, on 13 December 1947, was No. 6256 and, as was entirely right and proper, the commendable decision was taken to name it *Sir William A. Stanier, F.R.S.*

Usually speed record attempts on land, through water or in the air must comply with often arcane conditions laid down by some regulatory body; speed must be recorded over a measured mile or kilometre with an average taken from two runs in opposing directions, the return run must be made within a specified time and there must be no assistance from natural agencies such as wind or gravity. Railway speed records require none of this; it is sufficient to achieve the required speed, even if only over a few rail lengths, for it to be recognized and records can be established by running in one direction only and, usually, downhill.

The LNER had almost ninety miles of track between Hatfield and Grantham with long straight stretches and gentle gradients, all suitable for record-breaking attempts. On 27 September 1935 the new LNER No. 2509 *Silver Link*, the first of Gresley's streamlined A4 Class 4-6-2s, hauled a special seven-coach train north from King's Cross to demonstrate to the press and company officials the locomotive's high speed potential. The main demonstration started beyond Hatfield, where *Silver Link* was accelerated to 98mph followed by 107mph at Hitchin. From milepost 30 (just beyond Stevenage) to milepost 55 (just before Offord, where speed was restricted by some tricky reverse curves) the train's speed never fell below 100mph with a maximum of 112½mph recorded at Arlesey (37 miles) and Sandy (44.1 miles), establishing a new British record.

On 27 August 1936 the *Silver Jubilee* streamlined train supplemented by the LNER dynamometer car was hauled southbound from Newcastle by No. 2512 *Silver Fox*. A record attempt was made on the 1 in 200 descent of Stoke Bank (some six miles south of Grantham) and 113mph was achieved but at a cost. Boiler pressure fell too much during the ascent from Grantham and the locomotive had to be thrashed for the record attempt; the middle big-end bearing overheated and disintegrated near Hatfield but *Silver Fox* limped slowly into King's Cross with its train of fare paying passengers. A new record was established, but only just, and resulted in yet more publicity, and more passengers, for the LNER's high-speed services. The LMS had to retaliate but, first of all, it needed its *Coronation* Class in service.

LMS No. 6220 *Coronation* emerged from Crewe Works on 1 June 1937 and, with no unexpected problems revealed during running-in, it was announced that the daily high-speed *Coronation Scot* service would begin on 5 July. A special demonstration train was arranged between Euston and Crewe on 29 June for the benefit of the press and everyone expected that something special was to be attempted. The *Coronation Scot* train was used, but with its intended nine-car formation reduced by cutting out one of the two kitchen cars, resulting in a tare weight of 253 tons (275 tons gross). Driver T J Harris was at the controls, as he was on *Princess Elizabeth's* epic runs to and from Glasgow, with J Lewis as his fireman and Robin Riddles on the footplate equipped once again with roller maps and speed diagrams.

Unlike the LNER, the LMS had no long straight stretches with gentle gradients; its nearest equivalent was Madeley Bank, starting 9 miles south of Crewe with 1¾ miles of 1 in 348 immediately after Whitmore summit, followed by 3¼ miles of 1 in 177 and 2¾ miles of 1 in 69, which ended just 1¼ miles south of Crewe station. At the speed required for a new record this section would be covered in around 40 seconds and, as events revealed, this was perilously close indeed. Nothing dramatic was attempted for most of the trip as its principal objective was to demonstrate the improved point to point timings of the new accelerated service, which were impressive enough, and speed never exceeded 87½mph until after Whitmore. The crew decided not to pick up water at Whitmore troughs to avoid having to slow down and, after taking the summit at 85mph, No. 6220 was fully opened out down Madeley Bank. Speed increased steadily to 94½mph at Madeley, 108mph at Betley Road and the maximum was recorded just before milepost 156. The next few dramatic moments were later described by Riddles.

'Basford Hall sidings 1½ miles away now; spectators from Crewe coming into view along the lineside; and the train still hurtling on at 114mph! On went the brakes, off the regulator; but on we sailed, with flames streaming from the tortured brake-blocks. The signals for Platform No. 3 at Crewe, entered by a reverse curve with a 20mph speed restriction, came into sight. We were still doing 60-70mph when we spotted the platform signal. The crockery in the dining car crashed. Down we came to 52mph through the curve, with the engine riding like the great lady she is. There wasn't a thing we could do but hold on and let her take it. And take it she did; past a sea of pallid faces on the platform we ground to a dead stand, safe and sound and still on the rails. We had set up a new world speed record for the steam locomotive.'

Riddles over-simplified the situation. Platform 3, a totally inappropriate destination for such a train, was approached by a trackwork complex that included three reverse curves included within crossovers with six entry and exit curves and, according to one observer, the speed on hitting the first was nearer to 60mph than the 52mph mentioned above. There was some damage but, other than a few broken rail chairs, it was limited to crockery and passengers, especially those who were standing at the time, but the latter all emerged without serious injuries although many were bruised, shaken and stirred. The track must have been in superb condition to withstand such an assault while *Coronation* was probably saved from disaster by the excellent riding qualities of the Churchward de Glehn bogie.

Riddles may have been wrong on another matter. The claimed 114mph maximum was taken from the locomotive's speed indicator, an instrument not usually accepted as sufficiently accurate for such purposes. Some experienced observers, including Cecil J Allen, were on board taking detailed timings and none recorded anything higher than 112½mph although, as this reading was seen at both mileposts 155 and 156, it is possible that 113mph was achieved in between, thus equalling the LNER's record. The perennial question is whether *Coronation* might have

An interesting view of City of Manchester *at New Street Station during February 1962 with the driver's immediate concentration seemingly on other matters*
(T J Edgington Collection)

gone even faster and the answer has to be 'probably' – but definitely not down Madeley Bank nor, indeed, anywhere else on the West Coast main line.

Whether or not a new record was established on the down trip to Crewe is immaterial as the up-journey, taking place later the same day, was a spectacular demonstration of the new engine's unparalleled ability to deliver sustained power as it was one of the fastest runs by a British steam locomotive. 100mph was recorded only once, at Castlethorpe (55 miles north of Euston), but the 158-mile journey was accomplished at an average of 79.7mph with the 135-minute schedule cut by 16 minutes. The average over the 150.1-mile stretch from Betley Road to Kilburn was 83.2mph, including compulsory slow running through Stafford and Rugby and from Welton, some 7¼ miles south of Rugby, the 72.15 miles to Kilburn were run at an incredible 88.9mph. The engine's ability to perform superbly on work more closely related to day-to-day requirements than any artificial record attempts was of greater importance to railway managers but probably failed to impress publicists to the same extent. It was, incidentally, one of the last occasions on which 100mph was recorded by one of the *Coronation* Class although it may have been reached on other unrecorded journeys.

In spite of the dubious authenticity of the new record claimed by the LMS it was taken sufficiently seriously by the rival LNER. On 30 June 1937 it arranged a special press trip from King's Cross to Barkston and, on the return leg, A4 No. 4489 *Dominion of Canada* made an attempt to regain the record but its maximum speed down

Stoke Bank was 109.1mph - a commendable effort that showed tacit acceptance of the LMS's claim. The matter rested until 3 July 1938 when Gresley carried out some brake trials with new A4 No. 4468 *Mallard*, the first to be fitted with a Kylchap double blast arrangement. The train consisted of three twin-coach articulated sets plus the dynamometer car and the record attempt was again made on the 1 in 200 decent down Stoke Bank on the return leg from Barkston. Between mileposts 92½ and 89¾ speed stayed above 120mph with a recorded maximum above 125mph and this clearly established a new record. Whether 126mph was actually achieved (as claimed on the plaque fitted to the locomotive by BR in 1948) is open to question and Gresley was never convinced that this speed had been reached other than as a peak; he argued that claims should be based on sustained speed over a distance. He was, perhaps, disappointed as preliminary calculations showed that 130mph was possible but this was frustrated as temporary restrictions through Grantham station prevented a long fast run up to Stoke Summit, from where the high-speed descent began.

There were no further speed record attempts by British steam locomotives. Maximum speeds were imposed during the war years when trains were much more heavily loaded; postwar conditions were not conducive to high speeds as maintenance arrears adversely affected track and stock and, by the time that matters had improved, all record attempts were in the hands of more modern forms of motive power.

1939 marked the 150th anniversary of George Washington's inauguration as America's first President and the event was commemorated by a World Fair staged in New York City, occupying a site of 1,216 acres. It attracted exhibitors from sixty overseas countries and had as its stated theme 'the way toward the improvement of all of the factors contributing to human welfare'. Seventeen acres, the largest area for any single subject, were reserved for an international Railroad Exhibit and, in 1937, resulting from the considerable American interest shown in the *Coronation Scot*, the LMS agreed not only to display a *Coronation* Class locomotive with appropriate carriages but also arranged for the train to complete a 3,121-mile tour of North America prior to Fair's opening date, during which it visited thirty-eight towns and cities. The full itinerary is set out in Appendix 4.

The LMS decided to send the very latest streamlined member of the *Coronation* class, No. 6229 *Duchess of Hamilton*, which was completed at Crewe Works in September 1938 as the last of the second group of five locomotives with improved internally streamlined steam passages. Reference to Appendix 2 confirms that it was released some three months later than the others suggesting, perhaps, that the decision to send this particular locomotive had been taken somewhat earlier. For reasons concerned more with public relations than availability, No. 6229 visited America in the guise of No. 6220 *Coronation*, with which it exchanged both number and nameplates. Keen eyed observers would have noted certain differences. The second batch was to have been fitted with the Hudd magnetic proximity detector system of Automatic Train Control which required a louvred ventilation panel just behind the leading left-hand buffer, while anyone close enough would note that the locomotive's true identity was stamped on all motion parts and wheels. The greatest difference was, of course, in the livery; *Coronation*, in blue with silver stripes, was striking

enough but all locomotives in the second batch, including *Duchess of Hamilton*, were even more magnificent in crimson lake with gold stripes. Both a bell and electric headlight were fitted to conform to American legal requirements, the light being faired into the front casing above the smokebox door with the bell positioned behind it and just ahead of the chimney. The LMS ATC system (which, in the event, was not fitted) was incompatible with that used in the USA and, as conversion costs could not be justified, *Coronation Scot* was restricted to a maximum top speed of 85mph throughout its tour. Stainless steel handrail knobs were a special World Fair feature and these are retained to this day.

Unlike the LNER, which introduced purpose-built lightweight articulated coaches for its high-speed *Coronation* service, the LMS began its competing *Coronation Scot* with standard coaches although all received special treatment both inside and outside. New coaches were designed which, following Gresley's example, were articulated (as are the modern *Eurostar* vehicles) and the prototypes were prepared for the American visit with a very high standard of decoration and upholstery. Six vehicles were intended to form the new *Coronation Scot* and these consisted of three twin articulated sets (with each two carriages sharing a central double-bolster bogie) and included first-class accommodation in the form of a corridor brake, standard corridor coach, lounge and dining car with the other two vehicles being a kitchen car and third-class dining car. (At this time second-class had been abolished throughout Britain but, curiously, railways continued to provide passengers with either first or third-class seats!) Two other carriages were included in the American train although neither were part of the intended *Coronation Scot* formation; these were a sleeping car (mounted on two six-wheeled bogies) and a club saloon. Fittings included a cocktail bar, full climate control (although this was to malfunction during the tour and part

The Duchess *in the exposed fells around Lunds on the Settle & Carlisle line with the 'Cumbrian Mountain Express' during September 1990* (Roger Bastin)

The Coronation Scot *streamlined and articulated train photographed immediately before leaving for the USA in 1939*   (NRM Collection)

of its complex system had to be isolated), double glazing, heat, sound and vibration insulation and telephone communication between each compartment and the kitchen car. The train, less locomotive, had a total tare weight of 262 tons.

It was first thought that two locomotive crews would be sent but eventually only one crew was selected, this honour going to Driver Fred C Bishop and Fireman John Carswell of Camden Shed who had worked together on many Anglo-Scottish expresses and both were recipients of watches presented by King Boris of Bulgaria, a railway enthusiast who had shared *Coronation's* footplate with them during his state visit. John Carswell was a 'passed fireman', which meant that he was already qualified as a driver and was expected to take over some driving responsibilities during the tour. F W Soden, a senior Crewe Works foreman, was responsible for maintenance and all were under the supervision of Robert (Robin) Arthur Riddles who, although recently transferred to the post of LMS Mechanical & Electrical Engineer, Scotland, had been Principal Assistant to William Stanier at the time that the *Coronation* class was designed. Colonel K R N Speir, in his capacity as the LMS overseas director, represented the company in the USA and had overall responsibility for publicity.

The tour got off to an impressive start. The train worked from Crewe to Euston where it was unveiled to the British press on 9 January 1939, attracting many favourable reviews. The locomotive crew then had the unusual distinction of being interviewed at Alexandra Palace for a television programme but, in common with all early broadcasts, it was both scripted and rehearsed and left nothing to chance! Lord Stamp presided over a farewell lunch at the Euston Hotel which was attended not only by the departing team but by representatives of those responsible for building the locomotive and carriages.

On 19 January the locomotive and carriages were hauled 'dead' from Willesden to Southampton Docks, then owned by the Southern Railway. The vessel chartered for the transatlantic crossing was the m.v. *Belpamela*, a

Norwegian-owned 'Belship' designed for transporting railway vehicles, having a broad beam and large clear hold fitted with permanent railway tracks and a powerful 150-ton capacity derrick. The Southern Railway laid temporary tracks to its new Ocean Quay, which were tested using the railway's heaviest locomotive, a *Lord Nelson* Class 4-6-0, before the *Coronation Scot* cavalcade arrived. The locomotive, minus smokebox doors, motion and other components (which were crated separately, together with spare parts and other materials) was loaded into one side of the hold, its tender and one carriage occupied the other side, and the remaining seven carriages were secured as deck cargo, the elaborate paint scheme being protected with a thick wax coating. Loading took longer than anticipated with the result that *Belpamela's* departure was delayed until 26 January.

Riddles then crossed the Atlantic in considerable style on the *Queen Mary* with the remainder of his team following on the *Aquitania*, which did not have quite the same prestige. Nevertheless, all arrived well before the *Belpamela*, which had again been delayed, this time by severe weather conditions, and did not arrive at Baltimore until 20 February, a further six days behind schedule. Before leaving one of the coaches had been draped with a white banner bearing the words 'Southampton Docks sends greetings to the USA by the *Coronation Scot*'. The ship was met by a goodwill message, this time on a black background with the legend 'U.S.A. welcomes "the Coronation Scot", Good Will Ambassador of LMS – Southampton and Great Britain' from the Baltimore & Ohio Railroad. Before unloading began the matter of 'flag etiquette' had to be resolved as it was considered appropriate for the locomotive to be draped with both the American and British flags – but which was to have precedence and, for that matter, how was precedence to be indicated? In this instance the USA, as host nation, had precedence and the 'Stars and Stripes' was therefore positioned on the viewers' left with the Union Flag on the right. As the LMS team believed this to be the 'dominant' position, honour was satisfied for both parties!

Unpleasant weather continued, as later described by Riddles in his Presidential Address to the Junior Institution of Engineers. 'Unloading took place in temperatures which varied from 74°F one day to 26°F the next. Ice formed on everything. It was intensely cold, and the first major problem arose when the driver (Fred Bishop) contracted pneumonia and was laid up for a month. I decided I would do the firing and let the fireman do the driving.' Pneumonia was a serious and potentially life-threatening illness before introduction of antibiotics with hospital admission and constant nursing care as the principal treatment option. Driver Bishop was unable to rejoin the tour until 6 April and only resumed driving duties at Syracuse on 9 April. In his absence John Carswell became the focus of media attention and gave some rather controversial interviews. He complimented the Americans on their track bed which, he said, 'was almost as good as the British', he was critical of the quality of the coal provided (with justification), disapproved of white signal lights as an indication of a clear road and expressed surprise and disappointment that the train's speed had been restricted to a maximum of 85mph. Riddles was an experienced driver of more than average competence and it was inevitable that he would do much of the driving; this was confirmed by his own accounts of the tour and also by recorded observations.

The complex process of unloading was completed by 24 February and the locomotive and coaches were hauled into the B&O's Mount Clare Workshops, where arrangements had been made for re-assembly of parts removed for transit, removing the protective wax coating, general cleaning and final testing and preparation. The tour would have been impossible without the enthusiastic cooperation of all of the American Railroads involved but the facilities provided and hospitality offered by the Baltimore & Ohio Railroad were exceptional. Once ready the train had an unpublicized test run before being displayed to an invited audience within Mount Clare shops on 17 March followed by a trial run for the Press on the next day, which was recalled by Riddles somewhat later. 'Our first day out with a trial run to Washington for Press purposes started at 6am and finished at 10.30pm. Unfortunately, British and American locomotives are designed to burn widely different types of coal, and that provided at Baltimore by our standards was little more than slack. We had to refill the tender at Washington, and I compute that on that day we burnt 11 or 12 tons of coal – or dirt! I admit to having done a little driving in lieu of firing.' (In 1877, John E Wootten of the Reading Railroad patented a wide firebox, designed to burn poor quality fuel such as culm or anthracite waste, and this was widely adopted on American railroads.)

The train was reversed into Washington's Union Station where the locomotive stood next to the B&O's massive *President Lincoln*, attracting the comment from its engineer 'She's mighty pretty, but a little small, isn't she'. On the return journey the train was stopped near Relay, Maryland, on the Thomas Viaduct over the Patusco River, built in 1835 and the world's oldest stone railway viaduct, where it was posed for Press photographs alongside B&O's 'Capitol Limited' headed by the streamlined *Bullitt* No. 5304. Further demonstration runs between Baltimore and Washington took place over the next two days, once again with many staged 'photo-opportunities' with modern American locomotives, all intended principally for the Press but also providing Riddles with an opportunity of seeing the very latest diesel-electrics at close quarters. Their impact had far-reaching consequences.

The World Fair organizers regarded *Coronation Scot's* tour as a major preliminary event and, not only did it receive a considerable amount of advance publicity, but there was one very important passenger throughout; Charles C Green, Director of Promotion for the Fair, had use of the first-class dining car, which was converted to an exhibition coach. His home town was Kent, Ohio, and the one hour stop there, as shown in the itinerary, was for his and the town's benefit. The tour proper started from Baltimore's Camden Station (quite fitting really, as the locomotive would spend much of its later life operating from London's Camden Shed) at 10pm on 21 March, the starting signal being electrically activated directly from the World Fair in New York. The locomotive performed well and the demanding schedule was maintained, but the tour was not without incident.

The first breakage was a manganese molybdenum spring bolt. There was neither a spare nor was anything available locally so, with commendable ingenuity, Riddles used a valve spindle forging, of similar tensile strength, which was turned down to size. On reaching Harrisburg, as early as 24 March, the firebox brick arch was showing signs of early collapse and would have to be replaced as the climb through the Allegheny Mountains had to be tackled. (The 10.8-mile climb from Altoona to the Gallitzin Tunnel achieved a vertical rise of 1,055 ft with gradients steepening from 1 in 58 to 1 in 40.) There were two spare arches available (each weighing around 17cwt or 865 kilos) but the first replacement was installed so badly that Riddles had the second made ready for fitting once the train arrived at St Louis. Once again reference is made to Riddles' own account.

'Meanwhile, three of the front rows of the bricks of the arch already fitted (at Harrisburg) were found on our arrival at St Louis to have fallen into the firebox, forming a fused mass. Although by this time it was 1am, and we had to be away by 9pm the next day, I had to insist on breaking up the fallen arch and getting it out through the drop-grate – no easy task with bricks that were white hot and too large individually to be dropped through the small opening without being broken down.

'With the job done by 4.30am, I got to the hotel, where from my appearance I should have been refused admission but for the magic name *Coronation Scot*. I had a bath and some sleep; up at 8am for another bath, and off to the train to get hold of the Mayor and to open the exhibition. (The Ford Motor Company made a car available for Riddles at every major stopping place.) To allow the engine to cool down we waited until 2pm before getting busy (installing the replacement arch), but there was still a pressure of 50lbs of steam in the boiler. Only the boilermaker (and not his mate) would go into the firebox, and there were only the boilermaker, our own mechanic (Soden) and myself to see the whole business through. In we went, and suffice to say that 3 hours of heaving lumps of firebrick, some weighing 25lb and others up to 80lb, inside

One of the Settle & Carlisle's classic views; the Duchess *crests the summit at Ais Gill (1,170 ft above sea level) during September 1990*   (Roger Bastin)

an engine firebox with 50lb of steam all round you, is an experience not readily forgotten! However, the job was finished by 5pm, and an hour or so later the fire was in again and all was going well. Another bath, a rump steak and a bottle of champagne, and bed.' (Riddles would have had little sleep as he was at the controls when the train left on time at 9pm.)

The tour was a huge success. *Coronation Scot's* arrival at all intermediate destinations was met by enthusiastic crowds with many would-be visitors waiting patiently for hours for the chance to climb on board. In all it was estimated that some 425,000 passed through the train during official stops on the tour with as many as 100,000 others turned away as time ran out. The train's success continued during the Fair, attracting more than two million visitors by the end.

The major part of Riddles' job had been completed and he returned home in May, expecting to return to the USA later in the year to bring *Coronation Scot* back to England but world events dictated otherwise. The outbreak of war in September 1939 had an immediate impact upon the availability of transatlantic shipping, with most cargoes being restricted to essentials such as food and military *matériel*. In view of its success during 1939 the American Railroads and World Fair organizers requested that *Coronation Scot* should continue to be exhibited during 1940 (the Fair continuing for a second year), offering to pay for reconditioning and, with no early prospect of the train's return, the LMS reluctantly agreed. Later, with the increasing effectiveness of the German U-Boat offensive, the LMS might have been relieved to have its property in safe keeping but by 1942 the need for its locomotive outweighed all risks involved in its return. It was taken from storage in the B&O Mount Clare Workshops, loaded on to the s.s. *Pacific Pioneer* and arrived at Cardiff's Queen Alexandra Dock on 16 February 1942, from where it was hauled to Crewe via Hereford and Shrewsbury. The locomotive re-entered LMS service still as No. 6220 *Coronation* (but devoid of headlight and bell) and it was not until one year later that it regained its true identity, at a time when both locomotives were in Crewe Works for repairs. As No. 6229 *Duchess of Hamilton*

it was based at Crewe North Shed until the end of 1942, after when it was allocated to Camden, where it remained until 1947.

The carriages were less fortunate. At the end of the Fair they were transferred to Jefferson, Indiana, and were on loan to the US Army Quartermaster Corps as officers' living accommodation. All returned to Britain after the war but, by this time, the *Coronation Scot* was no longer and the carriages were used on more mundane duties. Many have questioned the decision to send the train to the USA when the political situation within Europe was so tense but such critics overlook the national euphoria that followed the meeting between the British Prime Minister (Neville Chamberlain), Mussolini and Adolf Hitler in Munich in September 1938. Chamberlain returned with a pact, signed by Hitler and himself, stating that England and Germany 'should never go to war again' and many (including Lord Stamp) believed that the problems of 1939 could be resolved without conflict.

Riddles returned to his duties in Scotland but in September 1939 he was released by the LMS in order to set up the Directorate of Transportation Equipment for the Ministry of Supply. This was a new directorate with far-reaching responsibilities not only for railways but also for inland waterways, docks and harbours, heavy lifting equipment, temporary bridges, sea-going vessels and innumerable smaller items. The directorate was responsible for some outstanding wartime designs including the 2-8-0 and 2-10-0 heavy freight locomotives, Bailey Bridges, 'Mulberry Harbour' piers and pontoons and the ubiquitous 'jerrican' fuel container. Riddles returned to the LMS as Chief Stores Superintendent in August 1943 but, in 1946, he was appointed to the Vice-President post, made vacant by the retirement of Sir Harold Hartley, with special responsibility for engineering policy. This did not last very long as, late in 1947, he was offered and accepted a new appointment as the member of the Railway Executive (on the about-to-be Nationalized British Railways) responsible for Mechanical and Electrical Engineering. (In effect Riddles had been offered the post of Chief Mechanical Engineer for the whole of Britain's railway system.)

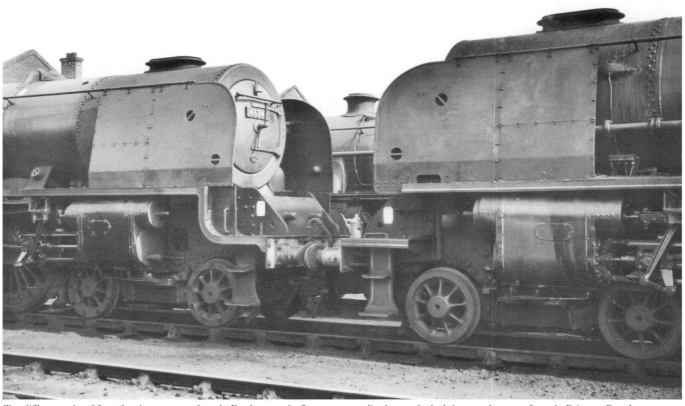

Two different styles of front footplates were used on the Duchesses; *the first non-streamlined examples had the curved pattern from the* Princess Royals, *as seen on the left, while de-streamlined locomotives and later non-streamlined examples had the cut-away pattern shown on the right. However, not everything is straightforward as both, seen here at Kingmoor on 6 April 1963, were built originally as streamliners. BR No. 46242* City of Glasgow *was extensively damaged in the disaster at Harrow & Wealdstone on 8 October 1952 and was repaired with the earlier pattern frames. No. 46247* City of Liverpool, *is seen on the right*

(*Chris Nettleton*)

The *Coronation Scot* daily service between Euston and Glasgow started on 5 July 1937 but the railway's initial lack of ambition resulted in disappointment. Trials with No. 6201 *Princess Elizabeth* demonstrated that a regular 6-hour schedule would be possible using locomotives with increased boiler power but, even with the new *Coronation* Class entering service, the advertised schedule was 6½ hours, although this included stopping at Carlisle. Four of the five 'blue streamliners' were delivered by the time that the service started and the final locomotive from this first batch, No. 6224 *Princess Alexandra*, was completed on 13 July. All five blue streamliners were used principally on the *Coronation Scot* and were first based at Camden before transferring to Glasgow (Polmadie) late in 1939, where they were joined in 1940 by three of the non-streamlined locomotives (Nos. 6230-2). Although others were added to Polmadie's allocation from time to time, these eight remained in Scotland for much of their lives and most were withdrawn from here producing a strange distortion in their mileage statistics. Glasgow-based engines were rostered more frequently on shorter distance duties resulting in average annual mileages of around 57,500, compared with 67,000 for the remainder of the class although there was considerable variation. No. 6222 *Queen Mary* achieved an annual average of only 55,723 throughout its life while the corresponding figure for No. 6239 *City of Chester* was 76,256.

An early performance test took place with No. 6220 *Coronation* hauling the normal *Coronation Scot* carriage formation between Euston and Glasgow, with the dynamometer car increasing tare weight to 331 tons (345 tons gross). About seven tons of coal were burnt during the 401½-mile, 6½-hour journey at an average of 39.2lb (around 18Kg) per mile or 3.03lb per drawbar horsepower per hour, this latter figure giving a much better indication of work actually performed. The average horsepower throughout was 825 (although this was exceeded at many places during the trip) which was well within the locomotive's competence, as confirmed below.

This result demonstrated that the new locomotives met the railway's revised performance standards and cleared the way for further construction. Ten more were completed during 1938, the first five, Nos. 6225-9 with streamlined casings and an attractive new livery based on the old Midland Railway crimson lake with gold 'speed stripes' and the others, Nos. 6230-4, were built as non-streamlined engines. (Reputedly, Stanier once observed 'that it is better to please a fool than tease him; they [i.e. the Directors] can have their bloody streamliners if they want them but we will build five proper ones as well!'. Nos. 6230-4 were clearly regarded, by Stanier, as the proper ones!) To many the non-streamlined locomotives had an impressive and dignified appearance that remained unsurpassed but others complained that, with their untidy assortment of sandbox fillers and lubricators, platforms above the coupled wheels resembled shelves in a ship's chandler! It was a design that benefited aesthetically from smoke deflectors as these hid the massive bifurcated steam passage casting around the smokebox base. It was envisaged, at least by Stanier, that ten streamlined locomotives would be adequate for the lighter high-speed long distance trains and that non-streamlined engines would be used on the railway's many heavy passenger trains but Lord Stamp did not agree. He believed that the publicity value of streamlining outweighed all practical disadvantages and streamlining reappeared on the next fourteen new locomotives, Nos. 6235-48, built between 1939 and 1943. The remainder were all built after Lord Stamp's death (April 1941) and Stanier's retirement (1944) and were without streamlined casings.

During 1939 consideration was given to reducing the number of express trains working north from Crewe by combining existing services, and trials were conducted to establish how well the *Coronations* could handle heavier trains made up of 20 coaches with a tare weight in excess of 600 tons. One of the first non-streamlined locomotives, No. 6234 *Duchess of Abercorn*, worked the first trial between Crewe and Glasgow Central early in February 1939 during which it was required to climb to both Shap and Beattock summits unaided by banking engines but it failed to maintain full boiler pressure and lost time on the hills. After being fitted with an experimental double blastpipe and chimney it repeated the challenge on 26 February 1939 and this time the results were completely different. With a train of 604 tons tare weight and 610 tons gross, No. 6234 was set a schedule of 150 minutes for the 141 miles from Crewe to Carlisle then 118 minutes for the 102.3 miles from Carlisle to Glasgow. The return journey, scheduled for the same day with no more than two hours allowed for turning and routine servicing, was to be accomplished in 116 minutes to Carlisle and 153 minutes to Crewe, with many of the 487 miles required to be worked at the extreme limit.

Its performance was spectacular. On the northbound journey the average speed over the 5.7-mile final ascent from Tebay to Shap Summit was 47.9mph and 36.8mph was achieved over the 10-mile climb from Beattock to the summit while, on the return journey No. 6234 averaged 63.4mph over the $17^1/4$ miles from Symington to Beattock Summit and 44.4mph over the $13^3/4$-mile ascent of Shap from Penrith. The down journey was badly delayed by track repairs but overall the net time was 10 minutes within the demanding schedule and, incidentally, within 90 seconds of that allowed for the 297-ton *Coronation Scot* while the *actual* time for the up-journey was similarly 10 minutes within schedule without taking up any of the allowances for permanent way delays. A record was established on this day, not for speed, but for power. Indicated horsepower (i.e. that generated by the cylinders) was estimated to be in excess of 3,000 over the more arduous stretches with a peak (southbound between Symington and Beattock Summit) of 3,300 while drawbar horsepower was regularly between 1,750 and 2,000 which, corrected for locomotive weight and gradient, produced a peak equivalent drawbar horsepower of around 2,600. All of this was achieved at a cost. While average coal consumption was not excessive at 3.12lbs per drawbar horsepower per hour, the highest horsepower readings were only achieved when consumption averaged 68.7lbs (over 32Kg) per mile and this firing rate was beyond the best efforts of a single fireman other than for a very short period. These results confirmed that the locomotives could generate power well beyond normal timetable or load demands and, indeed, that their firebox limit was well in excess of normal firing capacity.

Nevertheless the results provided convincing evidence that the *Coronations*' performance could be improved by double blastpipes and chimneys and these were fitted both to all new locomotives and to those already in service as they came into Crewe Works for repairs. (The draught of hot gases from the fire through the boiler tubes is 'driven' by a partial vacuum in the smokebox caused by the venturi effect of the exhaust blast. Experiments revealed that gases are not mixed into the body of the exhaust column but are entrained around its surface; the doubled

Duchess of Hamilton *at Blea Moor with the 'St. John's Peak express' on 6 April 1991*
(Roger Bastin)

No. 6234 Duchess of Abercorn *was photographed prior to trials held late in February 1939 when, fitted with a double chimney, it achieved an indicated horsepower of 3,300, the highest ever by any British express passenger locomotive* *(Gresley Society)*

blastpipe orifice therefore doubles the surface area for entrainment, increasing the draught and reducing back pressure from exhaust steam as it is forced out from the cylinders, both effects improving both steaming and efficiency.) As this exhaust escapes at a lower pressure, non-streamlined (and, later, de-streamlined) engines were fitted with smoke deflectors to prevent the softer exhaust from drifting in front of the cab. This draughting modification was the only important alteration made to the class. Two other minor modifications are of interest.

Gresley's 3-cylinder LNER locomotives used a derived or conjugated motion, taken from the outside cylinder valve spindles, to actuate the middle cylinder valve through a 'two-to-one' lever. At speed, whip within this lever caused the middle valve to over-run, a situation made worse by accumulated pin joint wear; with the result that the middle cylinder performed a disproportionate amount of work, submitting the middle big end to excessive stress. From 1938 drivers received advance warning of overheating big ends by a simple olfactory tell-tale device (sometimes referred to as a 'stink bomb') consisting of a volatile liquid sealed within a thin glass ampoule fitted into a hole drilled into the middle crank pin. The liquid volatilized with increasing temperature, eventually breaking the glass and releasing the strong-smelling vapour thus warning the crew of impending danger. Liquefied hydrogen sulphide was once used but the resultant 'bad eggs' smell was so persistent that locomotives were taken out of service for overheating for a day or two after the fault had been rectified. Acetone was then used as a substitute and, later still, it is believed that aniseed oil was used as its smell was suitably penetrating and, at the time, it was relatively inexpensive. In the late 1940s the inside big ends of larger LMS locomotives were giving rise to concern due to overheating and, while the cause may have been different, the LNER's solution was tried and found effective. Between May 1950 and March 1954 all of the *Duchesses* were modified and for very small outlay (£683 for

a programme involving 364 ex-LMS locomotives) many expensive big ends escaped destruction.

From the 1930s onwards the LMS experimented with speed indicators and recorders and such instruments, usually specially fitted, were used during the various high speed trials but widespread fitting was delayed by wartime shortages of precision equipment. In August 1957 it was announced that 'in view of the increased number of high-speed trains now operating in this Region (i.e. the London Midland), it has been decided to fit speed indicators *as quickly as possible* to the ex-LMS 4-6-2s'. The selected equipment was of the Smith-Stone pattern and all *Duchesses* not currently fitted were called into Crewe Works especially for the equipment to be installed. This apparent urgency is difficult to explain as general installation of speed indicators on other BR principal express passenger steam locomotives was delayed until May 1959; this latter project terminated well before completion due to 'the accelerated rate of steam locomotive withdrawals'.

The different topography of the two sides of Britain gave the LNER the edge in operating the very fastest trains but the sustained power of the *Coronation* Class was used in a way that was of benefit to many more passengers. In the summer of 1939 British railways operated a daily average of over 12,000 miles at speeds of 60mph or over with the LMS running almost three times as many such trains than the LNER. The much vaunted GWR had less than the LNER and the Southern had none at all; its fastest services had no start-to-stop speeds exceeding 58mph but everything changed after declaration of war in September 1939.

The *Coronations'* power was put to good use during the war years. The proposal to combine express trains north of Crewe had been dropped but while twenty-carriage wartime trains were common enough throughout the LMS, the general deceleration imposed by the Government meant that there was to be no repeat of the achievements of 1939. As maintenance became more difficult the elaborate peacetime livery gave way to an

'Dirty black streamliners had no publicity value…'. Duchess of Hamilton, *as LMS No. 6229, was photographed at Crewe North in 1947, soon before de-streamlining*

(Gresley Society)

all-over matt black finish that was uninspiring when clean and, when dirty, completely ruined the locomotives' appearance. Dirty black streamliners had no publicity value and, with reduced operating speeds, they can have been few voices raised against the decision to remove the streamlined casings. Postwar matters began to improve and Crewe began turning out repaired de-streamlined locomotives in gloss black livery with a simple but elegant style of lining. Even during the darkest years of the war, when every possible railway locomotive was used on whatever duty was required, the *Coronations* retained their place as the railway's principal passenger engine and it was only much later, toward the very end of their careers, that they were relegated to parcels, fitted goods and milk trains.

In 1948 one of the first actions of the newly formed British Railways was to arrange a series of interchange trials to determine which features of existing steam locomotive designs might be suitable for further development and incorporated into new designs. Trials involved selected classes, taken from regular working links, with each locomotive having run 15,000 to 20,000 miles since its last general overhaul and, to ensure standard conditions, fuel was to be uniform throughout each of the three groups to be evaluated. These were express passenger, mixed traffic and heavy goods and fourteen classes were involved, representing the four pre-Nationalization companies together with the 2-8-0 and 2-10-0 heavy goods engines built for the War Department. In the express passenger trials the London Midland Region was represented by the *Duchess* (this name was widely adopted by this time) and the *Rebuilt Royal Scot* classes, the Western Region by the *King* Class 4-6-0s, the Eastern Region by the A4 Class 4-6-2s

The final LMS Duchess, *No. 46256* Sir William Stanier FRS, *arrives at Crewe on 1 August 1964 with the 0820 service from Workington*

(T J Edgington Collection)

and the Southern Region's representative was the *Merchant Navy* Class 4-6-2s. These trials were conducted using Grade 1A South Kirkby 'hards' coal but this was to the disadvantage of the Western Region's representative and some tests were repeated later using softer 'Abergorki' coking coal from South Wales.

No. 46236 *City of Bradford* was used throughout the trials which involved working normal service express trains over the principal routes of all four English regions (only mixed traffic and goods engine exchanges took place on the Scottish Region). As many Southern Region lines were electrified using the third rail system there were no water troughs and, to compensate, No. 46236 was paired with an 8-wheeled 5,000-gallon tender from a WD 2-8-0 while running between London (Waterloo) and Exeter. Other routes selected for the exchanges were between King's Cross and Leeds (Eastern), Euston and Carlisle (London Midland) and Paddington and Plymouth (Western).

City of Bradford performed reliably enough but generally it was a disappointment as its driver seemed determined to demonstrate economy rather than power. There were occasions, especially between Exeter and Waterloo, when he 'took liberties with his point-to-point timing' allowing his speed to fall while climbing the more severe gradients then recovering the loss by fast downhill running, thereby reducing fuel consumption rather artificially to between 41.67 and 44.09lbs/mile or between 3.04 and 3.24lbs per drawbar horsepower per hour with an average of 3.12lbs. The LNER A4 4-6-2s managed even better at 3.06lbs while the GWR *King* Class showed good economy at 3.10lbs, but only in repeat tests using softer Welsh coal. In the first series of tests No. 46236 showed that it had by far the most efficient boiler as it was able to evaporate 8.67lbs of water from every pound of coal but, in the second series of tests using Abergorki coal (with a slightly higher calorific value), the *Kings'* boiler proved superior with 9.15lbs. It came as something of a surprise to many, but should have been less so when considering the driver's apparent intentions, that *City of Bradford* was not consistent in exerting the highest horsepower in hill climbing and, in fact, only topped the 'league table' on four out of twenty opportunities. On the Eastern Region's 1 in 91 gradient between Wakefield and Ardsley it recorded 1,775 equivalent drawbar horsepower and, on the Western Region, readings were 1,865 on the 1 in 57 section of Dainton Bank, 1,817 on the 1 in 54 length of Rattery Bank and 1,825 while on the 1 in 140 Bruton Bank on the return from Plymouth to Paddington. While remembering *Duchess of Abercorn's* 1939 exploits LMR personnel must have been mortified to find a *Duchess* beaten into third place during the northbound ascent to Shap Summit with the Southern Region's *Merchant Navy* 4-6-2 leading the way with 1,835 e.d.h.p compared with No. 46236's best recording of 1,506.

City of Bradford's uninspired performances did little to dampen Riddles' enthusiasm for the class as his original proposals for BR's standard designs included an improved *Duchess* with bar instead of plate frames but this idea was

The last Duchess *of all, completed by British Railways in 1948 as No. 46257* City of Salford, *waits at Carlisle Station to take over the 1400 Manchester to Glasgow express on 22 August 1964. The 25 kv catenary system south of Crewe was energised from September 1964 and, in preparation, all remaining steam locomotives prohibited by their height from working 'under the wires' received a broad yellow diagonal band on their cabsides* (T J Edgington Collection)

Specially prepared for working the RCTS 'East Midlander' special on 9 May 1964, No. 46251 City of Nottingham *was photographed at Swindon*

(T J Edgington Collection)

dropped as there were already sufficient powerful express locomotives to meet immediate needs. His policy was revised after No. 46202 *Princess Anne* was damaged beyond economic repair at Harrow & Wealdstone in October 1952 and resulted in construction of No. 71000 *Duke of Gloucester* in 1954 as a replacement but this was a very different design to the *Duchesses*. Any intentions of using this as a prototype for a new class were dashed in 1955 when BR's Modernization Plan was published, as this presaged an early end to mainline steam.

The *Coronation Scot* service was suspended during the war and never re-introduced but, with things beginning to improve after years of neglect, BR introduced the *Caledonian* in June 1957, which was a light-weight high-speed train between Euston and Glasgow with a scheduled journey time of 6 hours and 40 minutes. On one early occasion No. 46244 *King George VI* brought it into Euston 37 minutes early, having covered the 299 miles from Carlisle in a net time of 245 minutes at an average of 73.2mph. The final part of the trip from Crewe was covered in a similar time to that recorded by No. 6220 *Coronation* on the return from its record attempt with a marginally heavier load (eight coaches with the same tare weight but loaded to 280 instead of 270 tons).

There was further confirmation that the *Duchesses* had lost nothing of their outstanding pre-war brilliance when, in 1955, No. 46225 *Duchess of Gloucester* was tested on the Rugby stationary plant. The various detailed test results confirmed that power outputs recorded during the 600-ton maximum load tests in 1939 had been observed accurately and were repeatable under strictly monitored conditions. The boiler was capable of delivering 40,000lbs of steam to the cylinders each hour continuously (this meant an evaporation rate of 4,000 gallons per hour), resulting in 2,250 drawbar horsepower but even when steam production was reduced to a constant 30,000lbs per hour, the hourly rate of firing was 3,820lbs of coal (1.7 tons per hour or 67lbs [29 kilo] per minute). This provided further confirmation that the *Duchesses'* boilers were extremely efficient, not only in volume of water evaporated

for each pound of coal burnt but also in their ability to continue producing steam, and generating power, at rates well beyond those required in normal service. An enlightened railway management might have seized upon and utilised this 'spare' capacity. *Duchesses* fitted with larger tenders and mechanical stokers could, feasibly, have continued to work the West Coast main line until electrification had been completed throughout without the costly interregnum of diesel traction.

City of Bradford's desultory performances during the 1948 exchanges were put into the shade when No. 46237 visited the Western Region for trials during 1956. As recorded earlier, Stanier introduced a number of GWR features on to the LMS and, while most were successful, low degree superheating was incompatible with LMS operating conditions. According to some reports he later wrote to C B Collett, the GWR's CME, advising him of advantages observed with high-degree superheat but nothing was done until much later, when F W Hawksworth, Collett's successor, showed rather more interest. By 1956 the *King* Class 4-6-0s had been rebuilt with 32-element superheaters and double blastpipes and chimneys (this latter development based on S O Ell's research at Swindon) and the WR wished to confirm the success of their modifications in trials against a *Duchess* which, as a development of the *Princess* Class, owed its ancestry to the *Kings*. In the event there was little to chose between the designs but No. 46237 put in some fine performances even while being driven by 'foreign' crews. Driver Harris and Fireman Tobin, both of Old Oak Common, hustled their 14-coach train (461 tons tare, 485 tons gross) over the often difficult 193.7 miles from Paddington to Newton Abbot at an average of 64mph to arrive 2¾ minutes early while, on the up journey from Plymouth, a 12-coach train (393 tons tare, 420 tons gross) was brought into Paddington ten minutes early. Drawbar maxima of between 1,400 and 1,500 horsepower were recorded during these trips, which were well within the locomotive's potential.

The *Duchesses* were designed to work unaided over

long distances and many achieved some exceptional daily mileages. Locomotives based at Edge Hill regularly worked the 387-mile return trip between Liverpool and Euston (the *Red Rose* was never a light-weight train and frequently exceeded 400 tons) while others achieved single journeys of 414$^{1}/_{2}$ miles when working West Coast sleeping car trains over the former Glasgow & South Western line (via Dumfries and Kilmarnock) on their way to and from Glasgow. After the war it became customary for locomotives as well as crews of Anglo-Scottish expresses to be changed at either Crewe or Carlisle but on faster trains with limited loads, such as the *Caledonian*, the same engine was used throughout. Heavy named trains such as the *Royal Scot* and *Mid-Day Scot* often had 500-ton loads and locomotives continued to be changed at Crewe but, right until the end of steam on West Coast main line, *Duchesses* were regularly achieving some exceptional non-stop runs. The longest, by a narrow margin, was the 301 miles from Euston to Carlisle (Kingmoor) where the train stopped (two miles north of the station) for a change of crew and routine inspection by examiners and wheel-tappers. (Some trains stopped for the same purpose at Carlisle No. 12 Signalbox, a mile or so south of Citadel Station.) The class was also in regular use between Crewe and Perth and from there they were used occasionally as far north as Aberdeen and, less frequently, they worked into Edinburgh (Princes Street).

Locomotives used daily on the fastest and heaviest trains must be expected to have their share of casualties and the *Duchesses* were no exception but all their accidents resulted from human error, substandard track or adverse weather; mechanical failure was never an issue. On 10 September 1940 No. 6224 *Princess Alexandra* suffered a boiler explosion after its inexperienced wartime crew allowed the firebox crown to become exposed (i.e. the water level fell to the extent that the copper inner firebox began to melt), resulting in the fireman's death and, on 5 March 1948 the same locomotive was involved in a similar incident at almost the same location (on the ascent from Glasgow Central to Beattock) and in this case it was an experienced driver who unfortunately died. There were two tragic derailments; on 15 May 1944 No. 6225 *Duchess of Gloucester* came off the track south of Gretna with a sleeping car train with the loss of three passengers' lives and, on 21 July 1947, No. 6244 *King George VI* was derailed at high speed north of Atherstone and five passengers died as a result. In both instances the track was found to be inadequate with earlier extreme winter weather held responsible for the second disaster. There were a number of collisions, some of which were due to driver error. On 21 July 1945 No. 6231 *Duchess of Atholl* ran through signals set at danger and collided with a goods train; both crew members were killed in this accident at Ecclefechan. In a similar incident on Grayrigg Bank on 18 May 1947 No. 6235 *City of Birmingham* ran into a light engine on a section of track occupied by a track repair gang, fortunately without any serious injuries.

On 16 April 1948 there was a tragic accident caused initially by inappropriate use of the communication cord when a passenger stopped a Glasgow to Euston express near Winsford, simply in order to get off and arrive home without further delay. The signalman fatally compounded this action by letting the *West Coast Postal*, pulled by No. 6251 *City of Nottingham*, into the section occupied by the stationary express and there were many casualties. Reference has been made to the double collision at Harrow & Wealdstone on 8 October 1952. This was caused by No. 46242 *City of Glasgow* running through signals while working to Euston with an express from Perth and colliding with a rush-hour commuter train in thick fog. 112 people died in what was Britain's second worst rail tragedy

Duchess of Hamilton *at Tyseley on May 6th 2006. This side of the locomotive remains in BR Crimson Lake Livery. Tyseley's No. 7029 Clun Castle is alongside*
(Ian R. Smith)

No. 46250 City of Lichfield, *magnificent in newly applied green livery, at Euston on 8 January 1958*   (*T J Edgington Collection*)

(in 1915 five trains collided at Quintinshill, north of Carlisle; 227 were believed to have died in the intense fire and 245 were injured) and, although badly damaged, the locomotive was repaired.

The premature end to the *Duchesses'* illustrious career was something of an anticlimax. The class remained intact until the end of 1962 but sixteen were soon taken out of service including all nine based at Glasgow (Polmadie) in the Scottish Region's purge of its remaining steam locomotives. The twenty-two that remained still saw occasional use on mainline passenger trains, often deputizing for failed diesels or on special excursions, but mainly they were used on duties including parcels trains and fitted fast goods interspersed by increasingly lengthy periods in store. Once diesel numbers had increased, and their reliability problems had been reduced, there was no need to keep even these *Duchesses* in reserve. Two were

taken out of stock early in 1964 and the remaining twenty were withdrawn *en masse* in September 1964.

An anecdote recounted by Colonel H C B Rogers provides a suitable epitaph for the *Duchess* Class. On an occasion when the West Coast main line was cut by flooding between Glasgow and Carlisle, trains were diverted via the Hawick route between Carlisle and Edinburgh (Waverley). The *Night Scot Sleeper* with a load of 500 tons was about to leave Edinburgh when the driver, based at St Margaret's and a dyed-in-the-wool LNER man with much experience of Gresley's Pacifics, was asked if he needed banking assistance over the difficult Hawick to Whitrope section but he declined, simply asking 'which is the brake handle on this thing?' The following day, when asked how he had got on, he replied that he had never been on a finer engine! There can be nothing more to add.

An unusual but impressive combination – No. 6226 Duchess of Norfolk *in crimson and gold with the former LNWR Royal Train. After being withdrawn from routine service, the leading vehicle was later in use as the NRM's Support Coach*   (*Gresley Society*)

All five blue streamliners were all at work by mid-July 1937 and these were adequate for working the relatively lightweight high-speed *Coronation Scot* services, on which streamlining would attract the most publicity. The railway's next urgent need was for powerful locomotives for its many other long-distance passenger trains which would be more heavily loaded. As these would be slower, streamlining would be less effective and with less opportunity to reduce fuel costs through increased aerodynamic efficiency.

This reasoning appeared to have been accepted as in the LMS motive power construction programme for 1938, finalized on 26 May 1937, Board approval was requested for 100 new locomotives at a cost of £568,750. The programme included 2-8-0, 4-6-0, 0-6-0 and 2-6-4T types without reference to further 4-6-2s, streamlined or otherwise. Then, on 27 October 1937, Board approval was given to a supplementary item requesting that in order to meet 'the increased demands for engine power likely to arise in 1938, it was recommended that ten additional Class 7P 4-6-2 express passenger tender locomotives ('Coronation' type) be built at an estimated cost of £138,000'. These were all completed under Lot 145 at Crewe Works between 11 May and 7 September 1938 and entered service as LMS Nos. 6225-34, the first five of which were streamlined and the last of these, No. 6229, was named *Duchess of Hamilton*.

No. 6229 was completed on 7 September 1938 at a cost of £11,302, so much below the original estimate that the Board's earlier concerns regarding streamlining

costs became meaningless, and it entered service on 10 September as a Crewe-based engine. As recounted elsewhere it was selected to be the LMS representative at the New York World Fair and it re-entered Crewe Works on 9 December to be prepared for its transatlantic excursion where, during this works visit, it exchanged its number and nameplates with No. 6220 *Coronation*. It sailed from Southampton on 26 January 1939 but the outbreak of World War Two in September delayed its return to Britain until 16 February 1942. Once safely back at Crewe Works its was returned to almost its original condition; the bell had already been removed on its arrival at Cardiff Docks (it would have fouled the loading gauge otherwise) and other fittings essential for operating with the USA (electric headlight and automatic couplers) were taken off but it still retained its assumed identity. During its stay in America it was regarded as a Crewe-based engine (if only nominally) and it was from here that it resumed its LMS career in March 1942. It was still in crimson lake (or maroon) livery at this stage, unlike most other streamliners on which their pre-war magnificence had been replaced by unlined matt black.

It returned to Crewe Works for routine repairs in March 1943 and, with No. 6220 in works at the same time, the opportunity was taken to restore the locomotives' proper identities and, on returning to work in April 1943, it was once more No. 6229 *Duchess of Hamilton*. During this visit it was fitted with a double blastpipe and chimney. In May it was transferred to Camden depot, just north of Euston, from where it was used on the heaviest wartime

Unkempt but otherwise in fine fettle and with steam to spare, No. 46229 Duchess of Hamilton *arrives at Euston with the 0943 service from Wolverhampton on 11 February 1963*

(T J Edgington Collection)

passenger trains. (Fewer civilian passenger trains operated during the war years but their capacity was often increased by the addition of extra carriages. The sustained power output of Stanier's 4-6-2s was invaluable during this time of national crisis.) Around 1945 its pre-war livery eventually succumbed and it also appeared painted overall in unrelieved matt black which, although an essential economy measure, destroyed the visual impact of streamlining. Its tender was de-streamlined by having its side sheets cut back and the valances were removed from below the tank.

Duchess of Hamilton was transferred to Crewe North shed in June 1947 and, in December, it went back into Crewe Works for repairs. At the same time its streamlined casing was removed (it was one of the last to appear more or less as built) and, as with other de-streamlined engines with double chimneys, it received smoke deflectors. It returned to work in January 1948 as a British Railways locomotive although it was painted in LMS lined black livery. A further location change came in April when it returned to Camden and, in July, its BR number of 46229 was applied. October 1949 saw its return to Crewe North shed and it was repainted in April 1950, this time in the blue express passenger livery, with black and white lining, adopted in the early years following nationalization. Aesthetically this was not a success, either on the *Duchess* class (as, by now, they were referred to as such) or on most of the other types to receive it; neither did it prove to be durable in service. No. 46229 returned to Camden in July 1952.

Replacement cast steel inside cylinders were fitted during a works visit in April 1953 and *Duchess of Hamilton* returned to work in a new livery. BR had abandoned the less than pleasing blue livery and had adopted lined Brunswick Green (similar to the GWR's chrome green) which gave a much improved appearance. During another works visit, this time in February 1957, the sloping-front smokebox, left over from its streamlined days, was replaced by one of more conventional cylindrical construction. This alteration may have done little for the engine's performance but its looks were dramatically improved.

The streamlined *Coronation* Class were designed for the high-speed lightweight *Coronation Scot* service between London and Glasgow but this was suspended during the war and never re-instated. Its replacement was delayed until June 1957 when BR introduced *The Caledonian*, a fast train with accommodation limited to 84 First Class and 120 Second Class seats. *Duchess of Hamilton* worked the inaugural train from Glasgow to Euston and during the year achieved some fine performances often within the $6^{1}/_{2}$-hour schedule of the pre-war *Coronation Scot*.

In October 1957 No. 46229 was fitted with a Smith-Stone pattern speed indicator, driven from a return crank on the rear left-hand crank pin through a suspended gearbox, and also with ATC (automatic train control) equipment although, by this stage of its development, automatic warning system (AWS) would be a better description. Installation of a speed indicator represented the culmination of comparative trials started by the LMS in the 1930s and preceded BR's more widespread introduction

Duchess of Hamilton *wends through woodlands (and tight curves) around Kirkham Abbey with a 'Scarborough Spa Express' during August 1984*

(*Roger Bastin*)

On a cloudless summer's day in August 1984 Duchess of Hamilton *crosses York's Scarborough Bridge on its way to the coast*   (Roger Bastin)

of similar equipment between 1959 and 1964. In the late 1950s the London Midland Region began to repaint some of its principal express passenger locomotives in lined maroon and, following a further visit for repairs in September 1958, *Duchess of Hamilton* reappeared resplendent from Crewe Works as one of sixteen *Duchesses* to receive this improved livery. The early BR emblem, known affectionately as either a weasel (or ferret) on a mangle wheel (or the cycling lion), had been replaced by a more dignified design which was applied at the same time. In October 1960 *Duchess of Hamilton* ended its long stay at Camden and was transferred back to Crewe North Depot for the last time. Since its return from the USA it had been used exclusively on the West Coast main line on everything from fast, relatively light trains to heavy stopping trains with loaded weights in excess of 500 tons and had undertaken its share of working Royal Trains, especially between London and Carlisle - one stage on the trip to Balmoral - but all this was coming to an end.

Under the direction of the Railway Executive BR had adopted a 'softly-softly' approach to mainline diesel traction and invested in a limited number of pilot scheme locomotives with the sensible intention of evaluating performance over time. A change of Government brought about the Transport Act of 1953 under which the Railway Executive was abolished and the British Transport Commission, impatient with the earlier cautious approach, introduced its Modernization Plan in 1955, committing public finance to a total replacement of steam by diesel and electric locomotives. The pilot scheme was abandoned and many untested designs were ordered in quantity 'straight from the drawing board'; some worked well enough but

others were so unsuccessful that they were scrapped some years before the steam locomotives they were intended to replace.

The English Electric 1Co-Co1 Type 4 (later Class 40) heavy duty locomotives were heavy (134 tons in working order) and underpowered (a maximum of 1,550 horsepower at the drawbar) but were among the most reliable of the early diesel-electrics and were developed from one of the pilot scheme designs. From May 1959 production versions began to appear on the West Coast Main Line and, although never intended as express passenger locomotives (maximum speed was 90mph but only 79mph at full engine output), they displaced the *Duchesses* from their principal duties. Early reliability problems with fractured bogies and traction motors and not infrequent fires reduced their availability and displaced steam locomotives often stood in as replacements but it was only a matter of time before the diesels' problems were resolved.

Duchess of Hamilton made its final move in BR ownership when it was transferred to Liverpool's Edge Hill shed in March 1961. Although displaced from the West Coast Main Line there were, at first, some important passenger trains to work and, in consideration of this, it was treated to a final repainting in June 1961 and appeared with a later style of BR's lined maroon livery. During the war years Gresley's LNER 4-6-2s had been called upon to perform all manner of unsuitable duties and there were reports of streamlined A4s having been seen on shunting duties but throughout this grim period Stanier's 4-6-2s had been spared such indignities as they were always in demand for their intended work. As more diesels came into use

61

there was less and less passenger work for the remaining *Duchesses* and they were relegated first to parcels trains, then to fast fitted goods (on which they did surprisingly well), and finally they were stored out of use.

Duchess of Hamilton was stored between October 1962 and February 1963, re-entering service to be gainfully employed on a variety of duties until being stored again in October. It was back in steam for the busy Christmas period and even found occasional express passenger work (on the up Heysham-Euston *Ulster Express*) but it was usually seen on the inevitable seasonal parcels trains and then, on 30 December 1963, it seemed to be all over. It returned to store and was officially withdrawn from traffic on 15 February 1964. Its final recorded mileage was 1,517,250 and, excluding the time that it was stored out of work in the USA, it had achieved a highly commendable average annual mileage of 67,241. During its time in service it had exchanged boilers seven times (it began life with boiler no. 10306 and was withdrawn with no. 10297 built in May 1938 and fitted originally to No.6225 *Duchess of Gloucester*) and exchanged tenders once. Its first was no. 9747 but from 1959 it was paired with no. 9802 (both were Type 'A') which was built in August 1939 for use with No. 6239 *City of Chester*.

There were many excellent reasons for the official preservation of one representative of the *Duchess* Class and this honour went to No. 46235 *City of Birmingham* as the city promised to display the locomotive in a new gallery within its extended Museum of Science & Technology. Once installed it looked magnificent and, every hour or so, it actually moved along a few metres of track but the power was either electric or hydraulic and not steam. There was

no justification for the official preservation of any other members of the class and *Duchess of Hamilton* (together with No. 46233 *Duchess of Sutherland*, the other subsequently preserved example) would have been condemned to the breaker's yard had it not been for the intervention of Butlins Ltd, the holiday camp operators, who had already bought two other famous steam locomotives during the previous year (Nos. 46100 *Royal Scot* and 46203 *Princess Margaret Rose*). The engines were displayed at different holiday camps to act as both visitor attractions and 'gate guardians'; *Royal Scot* at Skegness, *Princess Margaret Rose* at Pwllheli, *Duchess of Sutherland* went to the Heads of Ayr camp and *Duchess of Hamilton* was displayed at Minehead in Somerset.

After its purchase by Butlins, *Duchess of Hamilton* first went into Crewe Works for cosmetic restoration, emerging in maroon livery as LMS No. 6229 and without smoke deflectors; it was well done and looked attractive but it was historically inaccurate as *Duchess of Hamilton* never appeared in this condition while in LMS ownership. (It was streamlined until Nationalization and, in its de-streamlined condition, it never ran without smoke deflectors.) However, a *Duchess* in inappropriate livery was far better than one in the scrapyard and even the National Railway Museum, which should be the paragon of historical accuracy, operated No. 4472 *Flying Scotsman*, after its acquisition, in LNER lined green livery (replaced in 1948) but with a double chimney (not fitted until January 1959) and trough-type (German-pattern) smoke deflectors (fitted December 1961)! Even Homer was allowed to nod, on occasions!

Duchess of Hamilton was displayed in the open air at

Soon after delivery from Swindon, where it had received cosmetic restoration, an immaculate Duchess of Hamilton *was photographed in the NRM Annexe*
(T J Edgington Collection)

The semi-cylindrical front skirting in front of the smokebox (*John S Hobbs*)

Minehead from April 1964 but within a few years its condition gave rise to concern as, positioned just a few hundred metres from the sea, there was no protection from the damaging effects of salt-laden winds and rain. Butlins Ltd did much to protect its investment; moving parts were greased regularly and bright metal rods and other motion parts were rendered even brighter with a coat of aluminium paint which did little for their appearance but helped in keeping corrosion at bay. As Crewe's glossy paint finish continued to deteriorate the locomotive became less of an attraction and more of a responsibility and, by 1970, Butlins were looking for alternative homes for their historic collection, with Bressingham Steam Museum taking *Duchess of Sutherland* and *Royal Scot* as early as 1971. Relocation of *Duchess of Hamilton* proved more difficult as any prospective owner had to overcome immense practical and costly obstacles before it could be moved. Eventually it was agreed between Butlins Ltd and the Science Museum (now the National Museum of Science & Industry) that it should be transferred to the then new National Railway Museum in York on a 20-year lease after visiting Swindon Works for restoration to museum standard.

This agreement was reached in February 1975 and arrangements were put in hand with many different agencies for its removal. The branch line from Taunton to Minehead was closed in 1970 but the track was still in place and a cautious trial run with a BR diesel locomotive confirmed that it could still be used. *Duchess of Hamilton* left the holiday camp on 10 March 1975 (its tender following the next day) for a fraught journey by low-loader to Minehead Station, a short trip made possible only by the full cooperation of local government and police personnel and with much use of steel plates to prevent drains and culverts collapsing under extreme loads. Preparation for the rail journey was the responsibility of volunteers from the Dart Valley Railway who lubricated everything that moved, and continued to do so throughout its journey. Rail

movement started on 13 March and was a slow and careful process; the locomotive had not turned a wheel for some ten years and, although some problems might have been anticipated, all went well although there were regular stops to check for overheating axleboxes and for application of ever more oil. The goodwill, patience and dedication of all involved in the move was rewarded by a safe arrival at Swindon Works on 17 March 1974.

It was decided that *Duchess of Hamilton* should be restored in its final BR condition. Re-streamlining was too expensive at the time and although it ran in LMS lined black livery after 1948, it retained the bevelled-top smokebox wrapper plate while doing so. As its cylindrical smokebox (the form in which it was withdrawn) was not fitted until February 1957 the only liveries that were valid were either BR green or BR (London Midland Region) crimson lake applied to some of the class in 1958. This was the selected option and with newly-fabricated smoke deflectors, much replacement steel plating and an immaculate paint finish, it left Swindon for York, being hauled via Gloucester, Stratford-upon-Avon, Birmingham and Derby. Restoration had taken over a year and had cost some £17,000. The locomotive was officially unveiled on 26 May 1976 at a dinner held to commemorate the 100th anniversary of the birth of its designer, William Arthur Stanier.

For two years enthusiasts were quite satisfied with what had been achieved but then the question 'what if' was raised. Could *Duchess of Hamilton* be restored to full working order, how much would it cost, how could the money be raised and would the locomotive be allowed to operate over the main line? The NRM itself was not the prime mover as its responsibilities are, and remain, curatorial but, without its full and enthusiastic cooperation and direct involvement, none of the events described in the final chapter could ever have taken place.

This view from Tyseley's gallery well illustrates the extent to which the streamlined casing extended in front of the smokebox (*John S Hobbs*)

The special relationship between the Friends of the National Railway Museum (FNRM) and the *Duchess of Hamilton* goes back almost as far as the locomotive's arrival in York and, until the NRM purchased the *Duchess* outright in 1987, the Friends made the payments to Butlins Ltd under the original 20-year leasing agreement. The FNRM, established in 1977 as a voluntary organization to support the NRM financially and otherwise in its aims and objectives, soon took its involvement further when a senior member of the NRM's curatorial staff, the late David Jenkinson, proposed that *Duchess of Hamilton* should be restored to main line working condition.

Late in 1976 David commissioned the celebrated railway artist Terence Cuneo (whose trademark mouse has almost equal fame!) to paint a portrait of the *Duchess* in its natural habitat, climbing Beattock with a heavy train, and arranged a limited edition of fine art reproductions from Manuscript, the specialist printers. Profits from their sale went into an account opened by the Friends specifically to fund restoration work but, inevitably, expenditure

'Partners' Day', 9 December 1989. Frank Paterson (left), then Chairman of the Duchess Appeal, receives the painting of the locomotive undergoing restoration from the artist, David Weston (second from left). Also present were John Coiley (right), then Head of the NRM and John Peck, who was the FNRM's Chief Mechanical Engineer
(NRM Collection)

mounted as work progressed but, as unsuspected problems became identified, the Friends' general funds were called upon.

A start was made in May 1978 when the *Duchess* was hauled out of the NRM and posed for sketches made by Terence Cuneo who, later in his studio, added super-elevation, train, scenery and the all-important smoke and steam effects, thus creating his hallmark impression of speed and power. The locomotive's overhaul then began and, as usual, every item of good news was balanced by the discovery of unsuspected essential work and, inevitably, of unexpected costs. The boiler and firebox were in good condition but all small tubes needed replacement; as these are 'consumables' this was only to be expected. Most of the flues (the large tubes enclosing superheater elements) and the elements themselves did not require replacing but the main steam pipe between the regulator (in the dome) and the superheater header (in the smokebox) had corroded badly and needed replacement while a hairline crack was found in the superheater header itself. At Swindon the hazardous task of removing all asbestos insulation from around the boiler had been completed so this spared one vital and expensive job but there were many others. Eventually, with all necessary work completed, *Duchess of Hamilton* was steamed on 14 April 1980 for the first time since its withdrawal some seventeen years earlier.

After passing all stringent safety tests necessary for

mainline running, the *Duchess* had a trial run on 1 May followed, on 10 May, with operating two trains around the York-Leeds-Harrogate circle, when the locomotive carried a 'Limited Edition' headboard, honouring those who had contributed to the restoration effort. Later that month the locomotive joined the Rainhill cavalcade commemorating the 150th anniversary of the Liverpool & Manchester Railway and, over the next five years, the *Duchess* worked a number of mainline specials, often venturing over routes never before visited by the class. On many it was accompanied by the NRM's support coach which, at the time, was Royal Train brake No. 5155, a clerestory-roofed veteran in immaculate LNWR 'plum and spilt milk' livery. *Duchess of Hamilton* made regular appearances on the *Scarborough Spa Express* but its exploits over demanding routes such as the Settle & Carlisle line attracted most headlines and, of course, there were opportunities for resuming its old acquaintance with the demands of Shap Summit. No. 46229's boiler certificate expired at the end of 1985 and, after a year that saw the *Duchess* working over the East Coast main line between York and Newcastle, followed by a 5-month stay in London (operating from its temporary base at Marylebone) it returned to the NRM as a static exhibit. During this 6-year operating period it covered 13,223 miles, very much less than its annual average mileage of 67,241 when in intensive daily service, but extremely commendable for a preserved locomotive of its weight and power with limited mainline opportunities.

Repairs carried out between 1978 and 1980 did not end the maintenance tasks required to keep *Duchess of Hamilton* in first-class working condition; much work was performed during the winter months between each year's operating season with many of the parts that make a working steam locomotive being replaced or repaired. Nevertheless the NRM's task after 1985 was immense if the locomotive was to be seen at work once more as, following expiry of the boiler certificate in October 1985, all tubes, flues, superheater elements and associated pipework needed removal before detailed examination and hydraulic testing (essential before recertification) could begin. (This is not excessive observance of safety regulations; superheated steam at 250 psi has immense destructive capacity if unleashed accidentally.) The cost for this work alone was considerable but additional repairs to both locomotive and tender were required. Available funds permitted an early start to be made on a project first estimated to cost around £50,000.

On its last day in steam Duchess of Hamilton *was photographed on the East Lancashire Railway on 21 March 1998 carrying the FNRM's 229 Club headboard together with its usual 5A (Crewe North) shed plate replaced by Camden's 1B* (Malcolm Tomlinson)

The NRM awarded 'flagship' status to *Duchess of Hamilton* and, relaxing its statutory curatorial responsibilities, approved work financed by the Friends to restore the locomotive once more to first-class working order. In this FNRM were advised throughout by the late John Peck, a respected former BR shedmaster who, in retirement, became the Friends' Chief Mechanical Engineer. The boiler was lifted on 6 May 1986 for transfer to the Oldham works of C H Thomson Ltd, who were contracted to complete all necessary repairs, which proved to be extensive. The smokebox was wasted to the extent that complete renewal was required, both tubeplates needed attention, the ashpan had to be replaced and cracks in the inner firebox, fabricated from $^5/_8$ inch-thick copper plates, could only be repaired by using specialized, labour-intensive and costly welding procedures. With the boiler

The new tender tank for Duchess of Hamilton *arrives at the NRM*
(NRM Collection)

removed, work started on re-metalling the coupled wheel axleboxes (the complete wheelsets were sent to Carnforth for this work to be completed) and on general repairs to both bogie and trailing truck, brakes (including rigging and brake cylinders), all pipework and spring gear, while many mainframe rivets needed replacing. Examination showed that the tender's tank plates had eroded and were little more than paper-thin in places. With little original metal to conserve (a primary objective of the NRM whenever feasible) it was agreed that a new tank should be fabricated with water capacity increased by 1,000 gallons by forfeiting space for 2 tons of coal. (Modern mainline railways need neither water troughs nor water cranes; working preserved steam locomotives therefore require enhanced water capacity and, with no opportunities for working lengthwise over long distances such as Anglo-Scottish routes, coal capacity can be sacrificed.)

65

While this work was in hand repairs to the tender frame and wheelsets were carried out. Another difficulty resulted from electrification of the East Coast Main Line as, in its original form, *Duchess of Hamilton* would not have been allowed beneath the catenary wires, so John Peck designed replacement cab side sheets, together with reduced height safety valves, reducing the locomotive's overall height to a safe 13ft 1in above rail level. (One of the original side sheets is displayed in the gallery above the NRM workshop.) New tyres were fitted with only one inch of metal (instead of the usual three) between the face of the tread and the wheel centre rim; yet another measure to reduce overall height but one that would have limited the distance that could be run before new tyres were required had the *Duchess* been in regular service. Boiler and locomotive were reunited on 7 March 1989 and, with other work completed, the locomotive was steamed for the first time after this second rebuild on 9 December, the occasion of a special Partners' Day arranged at the NRM for all who had supported the restoration appeal. A successful steam test took place five days later in the presence of BR's boiler inspector and a boiler certificate was issued. (From this moment onwards the 'restoration clock' began ticking; whether a locomotive is in steam or not, its certificate is for a finite period and can not be extended without further examination as time is one of the factors governing corrosion rate.) On 28 March 1990 *Duchess of Hamilton* ran light to Derby for weighing and adjustment of springs (to correct any weight distribution irregularities) and, after running with a load to Sheffield on the following day, it was awarded its BR main line certificate. The overhaul was now effectively and successfully completed; it had taken around five years and the final cost to the FNRM was £225,000. The means adopted to raise this amount, well in excess of early predictions, are worthy of mention.

1988 had been *Mallard's* year. Gresley's streamlined A4 locomotive returned to main line working as LNER No. 4468 and its various tours earned around £60,000 for the Friends of the NRM to add to the money raised by the first series of *Duchess of Hamilton* trips and much of this became available for restoration work. (There was a certain irony in using money generated by a former LNER locomotive for the *Duchess* which, in many ways, might be considered as a rival.) Once again funds were raised through sales of high quality reproductions of a painting donated by another celebrated railway artist, David Weston, who began work on his portrait of the *Duchess* under restoration in the NRM workshop on 14 April 1989. David's finished painting was displayed at the Partners' Day event referred to above. A very important source of recurring income resulted from the Partnership Project, an initiative introduced by Frank Paterson, who had recently retired from a senior management position with BR. Some 377 members of the FNRM each committed a minimum of £100 to the restoration appeal during its first 12 months and, by so doing, became Partners. However, as work progressed and initial cost estimates were seen to be extremely optimistic, Frank called upon the Partners for their continued financial support; this resulted in formation of the '229 Club'. Members undertook to contribute £100 annually or £10 monthly by bankers order and, through their continued generosity and that of the original Partners, almost £100,000 was raised towards the appeal, with many increasing their contributions to ensure that the *Duchess* had the longest possible working life.

Duchess of Hamilton returned to work on Good Friday, 13 April 1990, with a 280-mile return journey between York and Carlisle over the demanding 'Long Drag' of the Settle & Carlisle line with a train of heavy Pullman coaches. Pressure of time had prevented final

Duchess of Hamilton *at work in the early years of BR. The photograph is undated but the sloping smokebox confirms a latest possible date of 1956 (Gresley Society)*

No. 46246 City of Manchester *at Birmingham's New Street Station during February 1962*

boiler painting but, while incomplete cosmetically, the locomotive was in excellent mechanical condition and a credit to its restoration team. By the time of its next outing over the Settle & Carlisle with the FSS Cumbrian Mountain Express on 4 July, No. 46229 had been fully restored to pristine condition and its outward performance was equally immaculate but, on the return working on 28 July, discretion had to be the watchword as lineside fires had become a risk; subsequent progress was described as 'dignified and stately'. Between working engagements (BR had changed the rules and drastically rationed the number of one-off steam operations permitted on main lines) the *Duchess* became a principal attraction in the Record Breakers & Workhorses Exhibition in the NRM's temporary Great Railway Show. Engine drivers, as a breed, enjoy their deserved reputation for being phlegmatic and are unlikely to indulge in the poetic muse but 46229's performance inspired Driver Johnnie Anthony of Skipton to write the following:

> *I've driven electrics that spark in the night,*
> *And dirty big diesels, loaded and light,*
> *But nothing compares with that number one,*
> *The gracious old Duchess of sweet Hamilton.*
>
> *She's quiet and gentle, like all ladies should,*
> *And drifting at speed, she's really quite good,*
> *But give her the gun up the old S & C,*
> *She scares folks to death, (even little old me!)*

Poetry critics might dismiss this as mere doggerel

but no railway enthusiast could doubt the sincerity of Driver Anthony's feelings after driving a 'real' locomotive over this route. (Driver Anthony's verse accompanied his order for the 'Duchess of Hamilton 1990' video and was later published in the *NRM Review*.)

Duchess of Hamilton continued working over Britain's main lines until the end of 1996 when its BR 'ticket' expired and then continued its career on heritage railways, making its final appearances on photographic charters on the East Lancashire Railway. (For these No. 46229 reverted temporarily to BR's Brunswick Green livery which, although correct for the period between 1953 and 1958, never suited the locomotive's majestic proportions quite as well as crimson lake.) It returned to the NRM in September 1998.

It was around this time that a dramatic sponsorship deal made the headlines (and front covers) of the railway enthusiast press, most especially *Steam Railway*. The operators of the Venice-Simplon Orient Express (VSOE) announced that they would be leasing *Duchess of Hamilton* for ten years and that the locomotive would be re-streamlined; instead of the company's usual Pullman stock, it would be used to haul a matching mainline train. (At the time this would probably have consisted of refurbished and re-liveried BR Mk. 2 carriages as their profile was more appropriate.) For reasons outside the scope of this account this proposal came to naught and the *Duchess* took up its prized position next to *Mallard* in the NRM's permanent display. The 229 Club, dedicated to extending the

Duchess of Hamilton *outside Tyseley Works on May 6th 2006. This view dramatically illustrates the 'surgery' required to the smokebox*
                                                                                                            (Ian R. Smith)

preference for a streamlined *Duchess of Hamilton* at work on the main lines rather than on display within the NRM may bring about a further return to working condition but that, of course, should it ever happen, is well into the future. As it is, there is already much to be seen, appreciated and admired.

Duchess of Hamilton left the NRM on 9 September 2005 for display at the 'Great Gathering' at Crewe held on 10/11 September and, at the end of the event, it was towed to Tyseley locomotive works (Birmingham) where the streamlined casing was to be fabricated from original drawings and fitted. The cost was estimated initially at £90,000 with the 229 Club donating £60,000 while £30,000 was raised through the fund-raising efforts of *Steam Railway* magazine and its readers. *Steam Railway* always supported re-streamlining as confirmed by the considerable amount of publicity given to the 1998 VSOE proposal; the magazine's editor has similarly supported restoration of other National Collection locomotives by launching appeals and *Steam Railway* readers have responded generously; over the years their financial assistance has been invaluable.

Re-streamlining has not been without technical problems. In a recorded interview, Bob Meanley, the Chief Mechanical Engineer at Tyseley, responded to questions raised by Richard Gibbon OBE, the former Head of Engineering at the NRM and confirmed that no compromises had been allowed from the original design, based upon drawings supplied by the NRM. Mr Meanley stated that this was vital if the locomotive was ever again to operate over the mainline system as, if it could be demonstrated that the design had been acceptable in the past, 'grandfathers' rights' might apply to secure authority for future mainline running.

However, some problems were experienced during interpretation of the drawings as few details of the 'crinoline irons' were shown. (Crinoline irons are fixed to boiler plates on all locomotives, streamlined or otherwise, and are points of attachment for external covering plates. They maintain the space between outer plates and the boiler proper that is usually filled by an insulating material which was, at first, wood but asbestos was adopted and, later still, glass fibre was used although, on his MoS 2-8-0s

locomotive's active life as long as possible, continued attracting funds despite the restoration of *Duchess of Sutherland* to main line operation but any possibility of early NRM support ended with its acquisition of LNER No. 4472 *Flying Scotsman* in 2004. This famous locomotive was saved from possible overseas sale by a massive public appeal based upon the NRM's assurance that *Flying Scotsman* would remain in steam for all to enjoy for as long as possible; the resultant burden has been considerable. With all workshop facilities dedicated to rebuilding *Flying Scotsman* the NRM has few remaining resources, financial or otherwise, for rebuilding *Duchess of Hamilton* and prospects of its restoration to working order retreated into the indefinite future. How then should the 229 Club dispose of its accumulated assets?

Re-streamlining was resurrected as an option, and support of the 229 Club was requested with the majority of members agreeing to this proposal. If re-streamlined, the NRM pledged to use the locomotive as the centrepiece of a special feature and many supporters hope that public and 2-10-0s, Riddles filled the gap with nothing but air.) Bob Meanley's problem was that the profile of the streamlined locomotive varied along its length thus making every crinoline iron different. Drawings were supported by computer-enhanced images from photographs taken at Crewe during construction of the prototype and the latter were of sufficient detail and quality to provide most outstanding details.

The streamlined front represented a problem not just for Bob Meanley but for the original builders at Crewe. On its own a simple streamlined front was not good enough, as access to the smokebox proper was essential for both removing 'char' and general maintenance. The streamlined casing had to be opened regularly and its rigidity had to be equal to the task with increased metal thickness as one obvious way of achieving this. Bob Meanley found that the fabrication skills necessary for working metal plates of the required thickness, size and complex curvature were no longer readily available and regretted that few such skilled artisans could now be found within Birmingham which, for centuries, was known as a city of 1,000 trades (many associated with metal-working). Such skill shortages were brought about by diminishing requirements and, as businesses closed, their collective expertise has been lost and their machinery sold for scrap (or, in relatively recent cases, sold overseas).

The skills remain alive, to a limited and rarefied extent, in Coventry (and those with any knowledge of traditional West Midland rivalries will appreciate this) where one-off prototypes are still made for selected builders of 'exotic' motor cars such as Aston Martin while the aero-space industry continues to demand some 'high-tech metal bashing'. Mr Meanley was able to call upon such expertise (one suspects with a degree of both professional and geographical reluctance!) but his problems were not yet over. He discovered, as did the LMS many years before, that the original smokebox doors could not be opened without mechanical assistance. While there is much surviving relevant correspondence, drawings detailing later modifications remain undiscovered. In this matter Bob Meanley has, of necessity, engineered his own solutions and, with this essential contribution together with his other re-streamlining work, his name, together with that of John Peck, should be included in any *Duchess of Hamilton* 'Hall of Fame'.

Another gallery view illustrates the 'slope' of the rebuilt smokebox, resulting in the inelegant filling below the chimney casting. This view also confirms that different crinoline irons were required to compensate for the boiler's taper

(John S Hobbs)

Appendix 1: Principal Dimensions of the GWR King and LMS Princess Royal and Coronation/Duchess Classes

DIMENSION	MEASUREMENT UNITS (1)	KING CLASS	PRINCESS ROYAL CLASS	CORONATION/ DUCHESS CLASS
Wheel arrangement	~	4-6-0	4-6-2	4-6-2
Cylinders (2)	number	4	4	4
Cylinder dimensions (3)	in x in	$16^1/_4$ x 28	$16^1/_4$ x 28	$16^1/_2$ x 28
Walschaert motion (4)	number of sets	2	4	2
Piston valve diameter	in	9	8	9
Bogie wheel diameter	ft-in	3-0	3-0	3-0
Coupled wheel diameter	ft-in	6-6	6-6	6-9
Trailing wheel diameter	ft-in	~	3-9	3-9
Coupled wheelbase	ft-in	8-0 plus 8-6	8-0 plus 7-3	7-3 plus 7-3
Boiler diameter, maximum	ft-in	6-0	6-3	$6-5^1/_2$
Boiler diameter, minimum	ft-in	$5-6^1/_4$	$5-8^5/_8$	$5-8^1/_2$
Boiler length (between tubeplates)	ft-in	16-0	19-3 (5)	19-3
Firebox length (outside)	ft-in	11-6 (6)	8-6	8-6
Boiler large tubes (flues)	no. x diameter	16 x $5^1/_8$	32 x $5^1/_8$ (7)	40 x $5^1/_8$
Boiler small tubes	no. x diameter	117 x $2^1/_4$	123 x $2^3/_8$ (7)	129 x $2^3/_8$
Heating surface areas:	~	~	~	~
Tubes and flues	sq ft	2,007.5 (8)	2,299 (9)	2,577
Firebox	sq ft	193.5	217 (10)	230
Superheater elements	sq ft	313.0 (8)	598 (11)	856 (12)
COMBINED TOTAL	sq ft	2,514	3,114	3,663
Grate area	sq ft	34.3	45	50
Working boiler pressure	psi	250	250	250
Nominal tractive effort	lbs	40,300 (13)	40,300	40,000
Weight in working order:	~	~	~	~
Bogie	tons-cwt	21-10	21-00	22-10
Leading coupled wheels	tons-cwt	22-10	22-10	22-6
Centre coupled wheels	tons-cwt	22-10	22-10	22-6
Trailing coupled wheels	tons-cwt	22-10	22-10	22-10
Pony truck	tons-cwt	~	16-00	18-10
LOCOMOTIVE TOTAL	tons-cwt	89-0	104-10	108-2 (14)
Tender coal capacity	tons	6-0	10-0 (15)	10-0
Tender water capacity	gallons	4,000	4,000	4,000
Tender weight, loaded	tons-cwt	46-14	54-13 (16)	56-7 (17)
COMBINED TOTAL	tons-cwt	135-14	159-3	164-9

NOTES

1. Imperial units are used throughout as this system was in use within the UK during the time that the locomotives were designed and built.
2. In all cases drive was divided with the two inside cylinders driving the leading coupled axle with the outside cylinders driving the centre axle.
3. Cylinder dimensions as shown represent diameter and stroke.
4. The *King* Class had inside valve gear that actuated outside cylinders through rocking levers. As described in the text, this arrangement was reversed on the *Coronation* Class. The *Princess Royal* Class had independent valve gear for all cylinders, other than on No. 6205 *Princess Victoria*, which, in 1937, was rebuilt to a similar arrangement to the *Coronations* and could always be identified by its large modified motion bracket.
5. Length between tubeplates was 20ft 9in on the first two examples as built; as mentioned in the text, this was reduced to improve steaming.
6. The *Kings'* longer firebox was narrower and fitted between the frames. On Stanier's (and other) 4-6-2s, a shorter, wider firebox straddled the rear frames.
7. As built the first two locomotives had 170 $2^1/_4$in small tubes and 16 $5^1/_8$in large tubes.
8. Heating surface areas within the *King* Class altered considerably with the introduction of high-degree superheating under British Railways' ownership.

9. As built, the first two had tube and flue heating surface areas of 2,523sq ft.
10. The original firebox heating surface area was 190sq ft before the rear tubeplate was moved forward to create an extension of the firebox in the form of a combustion chamber.
11. As built the first pair had Swindon-type low-degree superheating with a surface of 370sq ft.
12. The final two locomotives, built in 1947/8, had 979sq ft of superheating surface.
13. The *King* Class was designed less to meet an operational requirement but more to restore the GWR's reputation as the railway operating Britain's most powerful locomotives. In terms of tractive effort, and this was all that mattered to the GWR's all-important Publicity Department, Collett succeeded admirably. Sustained boiler power was a factor of less interest to the publicists but, even against this more representational parameter, Collett's design would have scored well.
14. De-streamlined locomotives had a weight in working order of 106 tons 8cwt.
15. The standard MR-pattern tenders fitted originally had a coal capacity of 9 tons.
16. Loaded weight of the 10-ton tender would have been around 54 tons.
17. Loaded weight of the de-streamlined tender would have been around 56 tons.

Appendix 2: The Princess Coronation Class 4-6-2s (see Note 1)

LMS NO. (2)	NAME	ENTERED SERVICE (3)	WITHDRAWN	NOTES
6220	*Coronation*	June 1937	April 1963	4,5,6
6221	*Queen Elizabeth*	June 1937	May 1963	4,5
6222	*Queen Mary*	June 1937	October 1963	4,5
6223	*Princess Alice*	June 1937	October 1963	4,5
6224	*Princess Alexandra*	July 1937	October 1963	4,5
6225	*Duchess of Gloucester*	May 1938	September 1964	4,7
6226	*Duchess of Norfolk*	May 1938	September 1964	4,7
6227	*Duchess of Devonshire*	June 1938	December 1962	4,7
6228	*Duchess of Rutland*	June 1938	September 1964	4,7
6229	*Duchess of Hamilton*	September 1938	February 1964	4,6,7,8,9
6230	*Duchess of Buccleuch*	June 1938	November 1963	10
6231	*Duchess of Atholl*	June 1938	December 1962	10
6232	*Duchess of Montrose*	July 1938	December 1962	10
6233	*Duchess of Sutherland*	July 1938	February 1964	8,10,11
6234	*Duchess of Abercorn*	August 1938	January 1963	10,12
6235	*City of Birmingham*	June 1939	September 1964	4,7,13
6236	*City of Bradford*	July 1939	March 1964	4,7,14
6237	*City of Bristol*	August 1939	September 1964	4,7
6238	*City of Carlisle*	September 1939	September 1964	4,7
6239	*City of Chester*	August 1939	September 1964	4,7
6240	*City of Coventry*	March 1940	September 1964	4,7
6241	*City of Edinburgh*	April 1940	September 1964	4,7
6242	*City of Glasgow*	May 1940	October 1963	4,7
6243	*City of Lancaster*	May 1940	September 1964	4,7,15
6244	*King George VI*	July 1940	September 1964	4,7,16
6245	*City of London*	June 1943	September 1964	4,17
6246	*City of Manchester*	August 1943	January 1963	4,17
6247	*City of Liverpool*	September 1943	May 1963	4,17
6248	*City of Leeds*	October 1943	September 1964	4,17
6249	*City of Sheffield*	April 1944	November 1963	10,17,18
6250	*City of Lichfield*	May 1944	September 1964	10,17,18
6251	*City of Nottingham*	June 1944	September 1964	10,17,18
6252	*City of Leicester*	June 1944	June 1963	10,17,18
6253	*City of St. Albans*	September 1946	January 1963	10,19,20
6254	*City of Stoke-on-Trent*	September 1946	September 1964	10,19
6255	*City of Hereford*	October 1946	September 1964	10,19
6256	*Sir William A Stanier FRS*	December 1947	October 1964	10,19,21
(6257)	*City of Salford*	May 1948	September 1964	10,19,21,22

NOTE

1. The first official name for the class was 'Princess Coronation' and, after introduction of the non-streamlined locomotives, the official names became 'Princess Coronation Streamlined' and 'Princess Coronation Non-streamlined'. After removal of the streamlined casings 'Coronation' became the official name for the whole class and the unofficial title of 'Duchess' did not appear until later although this was to receive widespread formal recognition.
2. LMS numbers were increased by 40,000 under ownership by British Railways.
3. All were built at Crewe. Many went to Camden when new, where, with Willesden, there was always the highest allocation until 1958. Others were based at Carlisle (Upperby), Crewe North and Glasgow (Polmadie) although a few were based infrequently at either Edge Hill or Holyhead.
4. Streamlined when new.
5. Initial livery was blue with silver stripes.
6. Nos. 6220 *Coronation* and 6229 *Duchess of Hamilton* exchanged numbers and names between 1939 and 1943 (see text).
7. Initial livery crimson lake (Midland Red) with gold stripes and black borders.
8. Locomotives bought from BR for preservation by Butlins Ltd.
9. No. 46229 later acquired for the National Collection by the NRM, York.
10. Built as a non-streamlined locomotive with LMS lined express passenger livery.
11. Preserved privately and returned to main line working order.
12. 3,300 indicated horse-power (i.e. power generated at the cylinders) recorded during 1939 trials, the highest ever by any British express passenger steam locomotive.
13. The first to be built from new with a double chimney; also the first (in 1945) to be de-streamlined. Now preserved as a museum exhibit in Birmingham.
14. Selected as the London Midland Region's express representative in BR's 1948 locomotive exchange trials.
15. Last to be de-streamlined in 1949. Initially all de-streamlined locomotives retained their sloping smokebox tops required to fit the streamlined casing. Cylindrical smokeboxes were fitted later, resulting in a marked improvement in appearance.
16. Originally named *City of Leeds* but *King George VI* substituted in 1941 for patriotic reasons.
17. Unlined black livery applied from new as a wartime economy measure. Eventually all of the streamlined locomotives appeared in overall unlined matt black; this had a most unfortunate effect upon their appearance.
18. Intended to be built as streamlined locomotives and, when new, coupled to already-built streamlined tenders.
19. Lined black livery, based upon that used by the LNWR, applied to new locomotives.
20. First to be fitted with the 'utility' open front footplate, later adopted as standard.
21. Design modified by H G Ivatt to provide better comparison with the then new LMR diesel-electric locomotives. In reality the modifications failed to improve upon Stanier's basic design.
22. *City of Salford* was completed by British Railways and entered service as No. 46257.

Appendix 3: Euston-Glasgow Non-Stop Test Runs with LMS No. 6201 Princess Elizabeth, 16/17 November 1936

Down run (Euston to Glasgow): 7 coaches, tare weight 225 tons, gross weight 230 tons
Up run (Glasgow to Euston); 8 coaches, tare weight 255 tons, gross weight 260 tons.

Distance: miles	Schedule: minutes	Actual Time: min. sec	STATION or other timing point	Distance: miles	Schedule: minutes	Actual Time: min. sec
0.00	0	0 00	**EUSTON**	401.35	360	344 15
5.40	8	7 24	Willesden Junction	395. 95	352	335 45
~	~	p.w.s.	~	~	~	~
17.45	18	18 55	Watford Junction	383.90	342	325 38
31.65	30	29 55	Tring	369.70	331	315 30
46.65	41	40 32	Bletchley	354.70	318	304 27
59.90	51	50 53	Roade	341.45	308	294 33
69.70	~	62 46	Weedon	331.65	~	287 08
82.55	70	68 33	Rugby ***	318.80	289	276 05
97.10	82	81 08	Nuneaton	304.25	277	264 33
110.00	95	92 53	Tamworth	291.35	264	252 58
116.25	100	97 38	Lichfield	285.10	259	248 37
124.30	106	103 36	Rugeley	277.05	253	242 25
133.55	114	111 52	Stafford ***	267.80	245	233 46
147.65	127	123 47	*Whitmore*	253.70	233	222 53
158.00	136	132 52	**CREWE ***	343.35	223	213 17
174.30	149	146 00	Weaver Junction	227.05	209	200 37
182.15	156	153 30	Warrington	219.20	202	193 34
193.90	168	164 55	Wigan	207.45	190	182 42
197.15	171½	168 30	Standish Junction	204.20	186½	179 58
203.55	177	173 36	Euxton Junction	197.80	~	174 42
209.00	183	179 15	Preston ***	192.35	175	168 55
218.50	191½	188 05	Garstang	182.85	167	161 00
230.00	200	196 35	Lancaster	171.35	158	152 07
236.25	205	201 28	Carnforth	165.10	153	147 12
243.55	~	206 45	Milnthorpe	157.80	~	141 45
249.10	215	211 38	Oxenholme	152.25	143	137 18
256.15	~	218 04	Grayrigg	145.20	~	131 22
262.10	227	223 06	Tebay	139.25	132	126 15
267.55	233	228 12	*Shap Summit*	133.80	127	121 50
281.25	245	240 05	Penrith	120.10	114	109 15
294.30	~	250 00	Wreay	107.50	~	99 12
299.10	260	255 24	**CARLISLE ***	102.25	97	93 20
307.70	268	263 27	Gretna Junction	93.65	90	86 10
315.70	~	270 38	Kirtlebridge	85.65	~	79 55
338.70	293	287 35	Beattock	62.65	66	62 29
348.70	306	297 06	*Beattock Summit*	52.65	57	54 20
351.60	~	299 26	Elvanfoot	49.75	~	51 57
362.20	~	309 25	Lamington ##	39.15	~	43 17
365.90	~	313 15	Symington	35.45	~	40 35
372.60	328	319 30	Carstairs ***	28.75	33	34 30
377.55	~	324 44	*Craigenhill Summit*	23.80	~	30 16
383.10	338	329 38	Law Junction ***	18.25	22	24 30
~	~	p.w.s.	~	~	~	p.w.s
388.50	344	336 34	Motherwell ***	12.85	16	16 50
~	~	p.w.s.	~	~	~	p.w.s.
394.75	~	344 03	Newton	6.60	~	9 05
~	~	p.w.s.	~	~	~	p.w.s.
401.35	360	353 38	**GLASGOW**	0.00	~	0 00

NOTES

UP and DOWN LINES: Early timetables for services radiating out of London always had the capital at the top of the table irrespective of geographical direction. For arrival times at destinations out of London it was necessary to look *down* the column and, when intending to join a London-bound train, it was necessary to look *up* the column to establish the anticipated time of arrival. Trains running into London still travel on the up line and those running out of London use the down line.

p.w.s: A temporary speed restriction resulting from track repairs or maintenance is referred to as a **permanent way slack.** Drivers **must** comply with these.

***: Permanent speed restrictions in operation due either to tight curves, complex track layouts or proximity to platform faces. Once again, drivers must **always** comply.

##: A severe slack (i.e. only very slow running permitted) was in operation at Lamington but only on the down line.

Bold capitals, other than at departure and arrival points, denote principal stations where stops might be made by most LMS principal express trains.
Italics indicate summits of the route's principal gradients.

Appendix 4: Itinerary of Coronation Scot's Tour of North America: March/April 1939

PLACE	ARRIVAL	DEPARTURE	RAILROAD
BALTIMORE	~	21 March 2200hrs	Baltimore & Ohio
Washington, DC	21 March 2300hrs	22 March 2130hrs	Pennsylvania
Wilmington, Del	22 March 2350hrs	23 March 1145hrs	Pennsylvania
Philadelphia, Pa	23 March 1220hrs	23 March 2145hrs	Pennsylvania
Lancaster, Pa	23 March 2310hrs	24 March 1130hrs	Pennsylvania
Harrisburg, Pa	24 March 1210hrs	25 March 0030hrs	Pennsylvania
Pittsburgh, Pa	25 March 0640hrs	25 March 2130hrs	Baltimore & Ohio
Wheeling, W.Va	25 March 2350hrs	26 March 1130hrs	Baltimore & Ohio
Columbus, Ohio	26 March 1530hrs	27 March 1230hrs	Big Four
Dayton, Ohio	27 March 1400hrs	27 March 2200hrs	Big Four
Cincinnati, Ohio	28 March 0010hrs	28 March 2100hrs	Louisville & Nashville
Louisville, Ky	28 March 2355hrs	29 March 2030hrs	Pennsylvania
Indianapolis, Ind	29 March 2330hrs	30 March 1430hrs	Pennsylvania
Terre Haute, Ind	30 March 1600hrs	30 March 2130hrs	Pennsylvania
St Louis, Mo	31 March 0100hrs	31 March 2100hrs	Alton
Springfield, Ill	31 March 2335hrs	01 April 1900hrs	Alton
Chicago, Ill	01 April 1300hrs	02 April 2100hrs	Michigan Central
Kalamazoo, Mich	03 April 0215hrs	03 April 1330hrs	Michigan Central
Battle Creek, Mich	03 April 1410hrs	03 April 2100hrs	Michigan Central
Detroit, Mich	04 April 0035hrs	04 April 2100hrs	New York Central
Toledo, Ohio	04 April 2300hrs	05 April 1230hrs	New York Central
Cleveland, Ohio	05 April 1515hrs	06 April 1230hrs	Baltimore & Ohio
Akron, Ohio	06 April 1400hrs	06 April 2100hrs	Baltimore & Ohio
Kent, Ohio	One hour halt	~	~
Youngstown, Ohio	06 April 2345hrs	07 April 1230hrs	New York Central
Erie, Pa	07 April 1500hrs	07 April 2030hrs	New York Central
Buffalo, N.Y.	07 April 2230hrs	08 April 2030hrs	New York Central
Rochester, N.Y.	08 April 2230hrs	09 April 1330hrs	New York Central
Syracuse, N.Y.	09 April 1545hrs	09 April 2200hrs	New York Central
Utica, N.Y.	09 April 2330hrs	10 April 1320hrs	New York Central
Schenectady, N.Y.	10 April 1530hrs	10 April 2100hrs	New York Central
Albany, N.Y.	10 April 2145hrs	11 April 1200hrs	Boston & Albany
Springfield, Mass	11 April 1500hrs	11 April 2100hrs	Boston & Albany
Worcester, Mass	11 April 2300hrs	12 April 1230hrs	Boston & Albany
Boston, Mass	12 April 1400hrs	13 April 1230hrs	NY, NH & Hartford
Providence, R.I.	13 April 1330hrs	13 April 2100hrs	NY, NH & Hartford
Hartford, Conn	14 April 0030hrs	14 April 1330hrs	NY, NH & Hartford
New Haven, Conn	14 April 1430hrs	14 April 2100hrs	NY, NH & Hartford
NEW YORK CITY	14 April 2300hrs	~	~

APPENDIX 5: ALLOCATION OF PRINCESS CORONATION CLASS LOCOMOTIVES, 1937-1964

YEAR	Camden/ Willesden (a)	Crewe North	Glasgow Polmadie	Carlisle Upperby	Liverpool Edge Hill (b)	Holyhead (b)	TOTAL
1937	5	~	~	~	~	~	5
1938	14	1 (c)	~	~	~	~	15
1939	19	1 (c)	~	~	~	~	20
1940 – 1942	12	5 (c)	8	~	~	~	25
1943	20	1	8	~	~	~	29
1944 – 1945	16	5 (g)	12	~	~	~	33
1946	15	6	9	6	~	~	36
1947	14	8	9	6	~	~	37
1948	14	7	9	6	2	~	38
1949 – 1950	12 (d)	10 (h)	9	7	~	~	38
1951	14	8	9	7	~	~	38
1952	15	10	9	4	~	~	38
1953	15	9	9	5	~	~	38
1954 – 1955	15	9	9	4	1	~	38
1956	15	10	9	4	~	~	38
1957	14	12	9	3	~	~	38
1958	9	15	7	7	~	~	38
1959	8	11	7	12	~	~	38
1960	7	11 (i)	7	12	1	~	38
1961	6	10	9	12	1	~	38
1962	7	9	9	12	1	~	38
1963	3	7	~	10	1	1	22
1964 (e)	3	7	~	10	1	1	22
1964 (f)	3	7	~	9	~	1	20

NOTES

(a) All *Princess Coronation/Duchess* locomotives allocated to London were transferred to Willesden after closure of Camden Shed in 1961.

(b) Both Liverpool (Edge Hill) and Holyhead had locomotives allocated on a temporary basis from time to time. This list indicates only those on permanent transfer.

(c) No. 6229 *Duchess of Hamilton* was nominally allocated to Crewe North during the time that it was in North America as No. 6220 *Coronation*.

(d) The reduction in Camden's allocation at this time *might* have been due to the appearance of Nos. 10000/1, the London Midland Region's pioneer diesel-electric passenger locomotives although, as these usually worked in tandem, a compensatory reduction of one *Duchess* might have seemed more realistic.

(e) The first 1964 allocation shows the number of locomotives in stock at the beginning of the year.

(f) The second 1964 figure shows the numbers remaining in September, the month when all remaining members of the class were withdrawn.

(g) The 1945 Crewe North allocation was Nos. 6233-6 and 6252.

(h) The 1950 Crewe North allocation was Nos. 46225, 46229, 46233-6. 46243, 46246, 46248 and 46252.

(i) The 1960 Crewe North allocation was Nos. 46220-1, 46228-9, 46235, 46241, 46248-9, 46251, 46254 and 46256. Even at this early date the depot had an allocation of seventeen mainline diesel electric locomotives.